ArtScroll Youth Series®

Rabbi Nosson Scherman / Rabbi Meir Zlotowitz
General Editors

Published by
Mesorah Publications, ltd

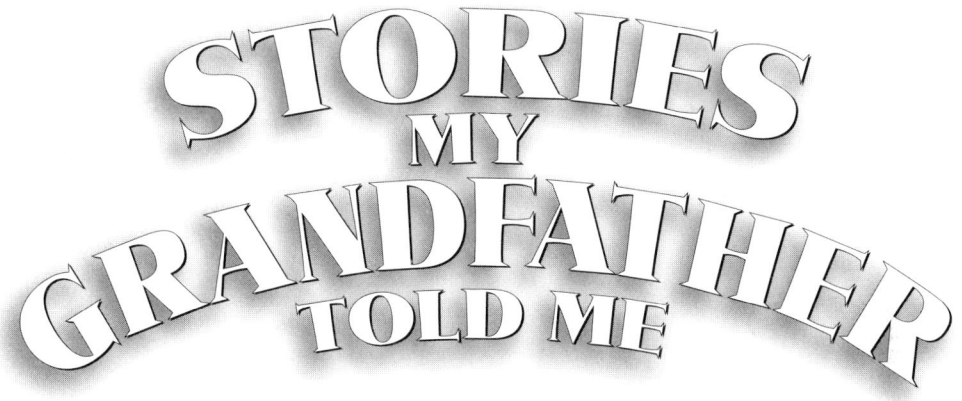

STORIES MY GRANDFATHER TOLD ME

Memorable tales arranged
according to the weekly *Sidrah*

VAYIKRA / ויקרא

by
Zev Greenwald

Translated from the Hebrew *Maasei Avoseinu* by
Libby Lazewnik

Illustrations by
Tova Katz

FIRST EDITION
First Impression ... March 2001

Published and Distributed by
MESORAH PUBLICATIONS, LTD.
4401 Second Avenue / Brooklyn, N.Y 11232

Distributed in Europe by
LEHMANNS
Unit E, Viking Industrial Park
Rolling Mill Road
Jarrow, Tyne and Wear, NE32 3DP England

Distributed in Israel by
SIFRIATI / A. GITLER
6 Hayarkon Street
Bnei Brak 51127
Israel

Distributed in Australia and New Zealand by
GOLDS WORLD OF JUDAICA
3-13 William Street
Balaclava, Melbourne 3183
Victoria Australia

Distributed in South Africa by
KOLLEL BOOKSHOP
Shop 8A Norwood Hypermarket
Norwood 2196, Johannesburg, South Africa

ARTSCROLL SERIES®
STORIES MY GRANDFATHER TOLD ME
VOLUME III — VAYIKRA
© Copyright 2001, by MESORAH PUBLICATIONS, Ltd.
4401 Second Avenue / Brooklyn, N.Y. 11232 / (718) 921-9000 / www.aertscroll.com

ALL RIGHTS RESERVED
The text, prefatory and associated textual contents and introductions
— including the typographic layout, cover artwork and ornamental graphics —
have been designed, edited and revised as to content, form and style.

No part of this book may be reproduced
IN ANY FORM, PHOTOCOPYING, OR COMPUTER RETRIEVAL SYSTEMS
— even for personal use without written permission from
the copyright holder, Mesorah Publications Ltd.
except by a reviewer who wishes to quote brief passages
in connection with a review written for inclusion in magazines or newspapers.

THE RIGHTS OF THE COPYRIGHT HOLDER WILL BE STRICTLY ENFORCED.

ISBN:
1-57819-529-2 (hard cover)
1-57819-530-6 (paperback)

Typography by CompuScribe at ArtScroll Studios, Ltd.
Printed in the United States of America by Noble Book Press Corp.
Bound by Sefercraft, Quality Bookbinders, Ltd., Brooklyn N.Y. 11232

Table of Contents

Parashas Vayikra

Tainted Tzimmes	13
Danger ... Theft!	14
Extraordinary Concern	15
Only the Best	18
The Unwanted Orchard	18
Panic!	21
In All Fairness	22

Parashas Tzav

Do Not Delay	29
Too Late	30
Efforts in Vain	31
In No Hurry	32
A Burning Hunger for Torah	38
Unknown Guilt	39
Gathering the Needy	40
Practice Makes Perfect	44

Parashas Shemini

A Strange Gift	47
The Seeds of Greatness	49
R' Chaim and the Fire	50
An Early Seder	50
The Case of the Switched Matzos	51
Overcoming Anger	53
Eating in Holiness	55
Mysterious Behavior	56
Breaking the Connection	57
A Bold Move	57
The Anti-Bug Campaign	59

The Correct Way to Answer a Poor Woman	60
Thanks for the Difference	61
Perfect Clarity	63

Parashas Tazria

Horse Sense	67
Compassion	68
Doubt	71
A Common Problem	73
A Just Compensation	74
Changing Fortunes	75

Parashas Metzora

"Stop the Coach!"	83
Humble Silence	85
No Atonement	88
R' Zusha Triumphs	91
The Gift	94
Hidden Treasure	95
The Day the Roof Fell In	96

Parashas Acharei Mos

Picture Perfect	99
Renewed Hope	100
The Proper Preparation	104
Heaven's Protection	105
One Mitzvah Leads to Another	108
A Just Reward	109
Six Gold Coins	112

Parashas Kedoshim

A Mother's Command	115
A Fortified Wall	116
Fair Wages	118
Extra Pay	120
The Case of the Missing Coin	122
Murder...	125
The Right Moment	125

Loving Strangers Like Family	126
"It Hurts!"	131
Man Is Like a Tree	134
A Source of Blessings	137

Parashas Emor

Honesty — the Best Policy	141
Just One Prayer	145
Business Can Wait	146
The Shabbos Shopkeeper	148
The Belzer Rebbe Takes a Stroll	150
The Test	151
Anticipation	152
Waiting for Mashiach	153
The Much-Blessed Esrog	154
A Beloved Mitzvah	154

Parashas Behar

The Mitzvah Garden	159
Human Error?	160
The Unseen Hand	162
"Eretz Yisrael Will Be Spared"	163
A Meal for the Rebbe	164
Enough for Three Years	164
Faith and Broken Wheat	166
A Personal Mission	167
Refugees	169
A Question of Borders	170
Everything Is Remembered	172
An Easygoing Boss	177
Pity the Prisoners	177
Rising and Falling	179
All Jews Are Equal	179
The Rabbi Is Watching	180

Parashas Bechukosai

Standing on Principle	185
The Missing Word	187
Satisfied With Little	188

The Miracle	190
The Policeman and the Drunkard	192
Compassion	193
The Apology	194
In a Hurry	195
The Best Preventative	196
Suspicion	197
A Cup of Tears	198
Special Status	199
The Tenth Man	200
The Bad and the Good	202

פרשת ויקרא
Parashas Vayikra

Tainted Tzimmes

וְהֵסִיר אֶת מֻרְאָתוֹ בְּנֹצָתָהּ וְהִשְׁלִיךְ אֹתָהּ
"He shall remove its crop with its feathers, and he shall throw it"
(Vayikra 1:16)
"But with regard to fowl, which [generally] takes its sustenance from that which is stolen ... it says, 'he shall throw [away] the innards' — for it ate from that which is stolen." (Rashi)

R' Chaim of Sanz ate little. He did not fast, but ate only enough to support his body and soul, "so that they do not run away," as he put it. He would taste a bit of every dish, then distribute the rest. His taste was very discriminating and he had a fine sensitivity when it came to food.

It is said that one Shabbos, when the *tzimmes* was served, the Rebbe picked up his spoon in order to taste it. Then he turned the spoon over and returned the *tzimmes* to its plate without tasting it. Everyone wondered at this, surprised that the Rebbe refused to partake of a Shabbos dish.

Later it was discovered that the carrots from which the *tzimmes* were made had been taken from a young gentile boy who, when passing by the Rebbe's house earlier in the day, had broken a pane of glass in a window. Members of the household caught the boy and took the carrots away as a fine for breaking the window.

Though the Rebbe knew nothing of all this, his delicate sensitivity sensed that the carrots fell into the category of stolen property, and he refused to touch the dish made from them.

Danger ... Theft!

וְהֵסִיר אֶת מֻרְאָתוֹ בְּנֹצָתָהּ וְהִשְׁלִיךְ אֹתָהּ

"He shall remove its crop with its feathers, and he shall throw it"

(Vayikra 1:16)

According to R' Aryeh Leib, his father, the Chofetz Chaim, resided in Warsaw during the printing of his *Mishnah Berurah*, in order to supervise the work.

"Because it is a *halachah sefer*, from which we learn what is forbidden and what is permissible," the Chofetz Chaim explained, "it is very important to make sure that no error creeps in, *chas v'shalom*. Also, the customer pays for a book that is well printed. If I do not supervise the printing to make sure it is clean and clear, I might, *chas v'shalom*, be guilty of stealing!"

It was not easy for the Chofetz Chaim to give up his regular learning routine or his scheduled *shiurim*. These were very precious to him. But he considered this job very important — so important that he would entrust it to no one else. It was only when his son, R' Aryeh Leib, moved to Warsaw that the Chofetz Chaim finally passed the task on to him.

After that, the Chofetz Chaim received a letter from a buyer, complaining that his copy of the *Mishnah Berurah* had several pages in the wrong places. He immediately forwarded the letter to his son, attaching a note of his own:

"See, my son, what you have done to me! All my life I have anxiously avoided even the suspicion of stealing. And now, because you were not careful enough, I have been guilty of actual stealing!"

The Chofetz Chaim sent the buyer a new *sefer*. Then he went even further, placing an ad in the newspaper offering a new copy to anyone who found misplaced pages in their *Mishnah Berurah*.

Honesty was paramount to R' Yisrael of Vizhnitz. He was scrupulously honest with Jews and gentiles alike.

A Jew approached him once to ask his advice about dealing in counterfeit coins. R' Yisrael was vehemently opposed.

"Every person has an angel up above who watches over him. The Emperor certainly has one, too. If people try to counterfeit the Emperor's image on coins, this angers the Emperor's angel and causes it to hand the counterfeiters over to the authorities!"

Whenever R' Yisrael sent a letter via a messenger instead of through the mail, he would rip up a stamp.

Once, when traveling by train, his aide and companions did not manage to purchase tickets before boarding. Because of severely crowded conditions, the conductor did not come around to punch the passengers' tickets. As they approached their destination, R' Yisrael suddenly asked, "Did you buy tickets?"

His aide was surprised; this was not a matter the Rebbe usually asked about.

"No," he answered.

"How can that be?" exclaimed the Rebbe. "This is outright theft! What difference does it make whether one removes a wallet from somebody's pocket, or steals in this way?

"The moment we reach the city," he concluded forcefully, "buy tickets — and tear them up!"

Extraordinary Concern

וְנֶפֶשׁ כִּי תַקְרִיב קָרְבַּן מִנְחָה לַד׳

"When a person offers a meal-offering to Hashem"

(Vayikra 2:1)

> "'Soul' was not used with reference to any voluntary offerings except for the meal-offering. [The reason for this is as follows:] Whose practice is it to dedicate a meal-offering? A poor person. The Holy One, Blessed is He, said, ['Although the poor man's offering is modest,] I consider it on his behalf as if he offered his soul.'" (Rashi)

There was once a Jew in the city of Stanislav who contracted a serious case of hepatitis that left his face looking strange and repulsive. Anyone who laid eyes on him would recoil in disgust. Because of his repulsive appearance, this unfortunate man was unable to form any kind of friendship with other people.

Once, when R' Yisrael of Vizhnitz passed through Stanislav, all the Jewish townspeople turned out to greet him. Among the crowd was the unfortunate man with the deformed face. He, too, wished to approach the Rebbe and ask for his blessing.

Seeing him, the others moved aside, leaving him a clear path to his goal. The man's pain at this treatment left him so anguished that, as he stood before the Vizhnitzer Rebbe, he burst into heartbreaking sobs.

But the Rebbe did not behave as the others had. He moved close to the crying man, embraced and kissed him warmly, and lavished on him more affection than he had to anyone else there.

On another occasion, the Rebbe came to the city of Chust, in Marmorosh. Here, too, Chassidim came out in droves to welcome the Rebbe. Among them was a Jew suffering with boils. Awful, disfiguring blisters covered his body.

When he approached the Rebbe for a *berachah,* the Rebbe embraced and kissed him with great love — until all those present broke down in tears at the sight of such goodness of heart, such greatness of spirit.

R' Chaika's *davening* was performed with incredible devotion and self-denial. Once, when reciting the words, "*Beyado afkid ruchi*" ("To His Hand I submit my spirit"), R' Chaika fainted. When he regained consciousness, he spoke to the men standing around him.

"A king once commanded his subjects to bring all their property to him. One of those who came was an extremely destitute man who carried all of his belongings in one small kerchief. Seeing the vast wealth that others had brought the king, the poor man broke down in tears, embittered by the knowledge that he had so little to offer his sovereign.

"I, too, seeing the lofty service that the angels and *seraphim* offer Hashem, and having only my poor soul, spirit, and service to offer Him, felt exactly like that destitute subject with his meager bundle."

R' Moshe Leib of Sassov once came to the marketplace in Yaroslav. He was passing among the vendors, checking the quality of the straw and hay for sale, when he met his friend, R' Shimon of Yaroslav.

"Rebbe, what are you doing here?" R' Shimon asked in surprise.

"Leave out my 'Rebbe' and your 'Rebbe' and come with me to carry a bale of hay to a poor widow who has no hay or straw upon which to lay her broken body."

The two *tzaddikim* went together, hauling a bale of hay on their shoulders. Astonished bystanders stared in wonder and moved aside to make room for them to pass.

As they went, R' Moshe Leib remarked, "Were the *Beis Hamikdash* standing today, we would be bringing sacrifices and libations. Now we bring straw — and it is as though we have all the *kavanos* (spiritual intentions) that come with sacrificing a *korban minchah*."

R' Moshe Leib of Sassov's father, R' Yaakov, would take a job grinding wheat at the mill — not for himself, though he was also a poor man, but for a widow and orphan who lived in his neighborhood. And he did this despite his great and abiding love for the Torah, which he learned constantly.

Moshe Leib, his son, followed in his father's footsteps. Despite his greatness in Torah, he did not worry about his honor when it came to performing acts of *chesed* with his own hands — even if they were beneath him.

Every Rosh Hashanah, R' Chaim of Sanz would *daven* for the congregation in the town's largest shul, and he personally blew the shofar as well. His prayers were earth-shattering and split the heavens. One Rosh Hashanah, when the shul was filled to capacity, a great number of men climbed up to the roof, above the women's section, to *daven* there and to be able to hear what was going on inside. Suddenly, the roof began to buckle.

Naturally, the shul erupted in a great commotion, as people tried to flee the building. The Rebbe continued to stand and *daven,* so devotedly and with such fervor, that he did not notice the noise or the panic. Finally, someone pulled him to safety through a window.

All the way home, the Sanzer Rebbe did not speak a word or ask what had happened. Upon his arrival, he went at once to his own shul and continued *davening* without hesitation. Hearing his voice uplifted in prayer, many of the people gathered in the shul and continued *davening* there as well.

It was only afterwards, when he had concluded *Mussaf,* that the Rebbe asked why they had fled the large shul earlier!

Only the Best

כָּל חֵלֶב לַד׳

"All the choice parts for Hashem"
(Vayikra 3:16)

The Gerrer Rebbe, R' Avraham Mordechai, owned a pair of tefillin that had been written by R' Moshe of Peshevorsk. These were very prestigious tefillin indeed. The Rebbe wore them only on erev Yom Kippur, apparently considering himself unworthy of donning them on any other day.

Once, a boy came to him and said that he had no *tefillin*. The Gerrer Rebbe took the precious *tefillin* and handed them to the boy. Seeing the boy put on the *tefillin* written by R' Moshe of Peshevorsk, the Rebbe's sons asked their father for an explanation.

"The Torah says, 'all the choice parts for Hashem,'" the Rebbe explained. "The Rambam says that just as we must offer up to Hashem the choicest parts of the sacrifice, so, too, when it comes to the mitzvah of giving *tzedakah* to the poor, we must give only of the best!"

The Unwanted Orchard

נֶפֶשׁ כִּי תֶחֱטָא וּמָעֲלָה מַעַל בַּד׳ וְכִחֵשׁ בַּעֲמִיתוֹ בְּפִקָּדוֹן אוֹ בִתְשׂוּמֶת יָד אוֹ בְגָזֵל אוֹ עָשַׁק אֶת עֲמִיתוֹ

"If a person will sin and commit a treachery against Hashem by lying to his comrade regarding a pledge or a loan or a robbery; or by defrauding his comrade."
(Vayikra 5:21)

R' Sholom Schwadron used to tell of R' Eliyahu Dushnitzer, *mashgiach* of the Lomze Yeshivah in Petach Tikvah, whose son, R'

Asher, had left him an orange orchard in Ramat Hasharon when he went to live in America.

A difficult period followed for orchard-owners and they suffered many heavy losses. In order to maintain his trees, R' Dushnitzer was forced to go into debt. He grew increasingly distressed over the mounting debts, and was afraid of leaving the world as a debtor, in the category of a "wicked man who borrows but does not repay." He prayed earnestly, and asked his friends to *daven* as well, that he might sell the orchard and so be in a position to repay all his debts.

One of his students, a married man, worked as a realtor selling apartments and lots. Through his efforts, an American man was found who was interested in purchasing the orchard. The prospective buyer, the realtor and R' Eliyahu traveled to Ramat Hasharon to inspect the place. On the bus, R' Dushnitzer sat beside the prospective buyer and said, "The Torah obligates us not to oppress our fellow man financially. Therefore, I must point out my orchard's defects. Worms have been found in one of the trees; a second has borne less fruit than usual this year, and a third is dry. Also, the *Gemara* states that a man who hires workers but does not work alongside them is likely to lose his money. This rule applies to all sorts of situations, especially in the case of my orchard, which already has so many problems. Therefore, I must tell you that if you do not work the orchard personally, you are throwing away your money."

The buyer listened patiently to all this, but said nothing. His attitude seemed to say, "No matter what, I'm buying!"

When the bus pulled into Ramat Hasharon, the three men went immediately to see the orchard. R' Dushnitzer began to point out all the defects he had mentioned earlier, on the principle that seeing is more powerful than hearing. "Here is the wormy tree, here is the dry one; there is a hole in the ground."

The buyer stood silent. His stance was unwavering; he still intended to buy.

They walked along, inspecting the trees. Suddenly, the buyer stopped. Taking a small bottle out of his pocket, he drank a few drops. R' Dushnitzer asked in alarm, "What's the matter?"

"Don't be anxious," the buyer reassured him. "It's just that I have a weak heart. The doctor has given me some medicine to take from time to time."

The words were scarcely out of his mouth when R' Dushnitzer

exclaimed, "May *Hakadosh Baruch Hu* grant you a speedy recovery — but I cannot sell you my orchard under any circumstances!"

The buyer's patience evaporated. "Why not, Rabbi? I want to buy it!"

"If *you* don't understand that this deal is not good for you, does that permit me to harm you? I've already told you that hiring workers without working alongside them is the path to losing money. Can a person such as yourself, with a weak heart, work a difficult orchard like this? Of course not! I won't sell you the orchard!"

R' Dushnitzer returned to Petach Tikvah at once.

A few days later, he met his student, R' Sholom Schwadron, at Tel Aviv's central bus station. "You have received some benefit at the yeshivah," R' Dushnitzer said, "so I feel that I can permit myself to ask a favor of you. You are aware of the aggravation I have been feeling over my orchard. Some time ago, I asked one of your friends from the yeshivah, a man who opened a Talmud Torah in Yerushalayim, to say *Tehillim* with his boys after class every day, to pray for my success in selling the orchard and paying my debts. I didn't ask him to say *Tehillim* during class time, *chas v'shalom,* in order not to steal any time away from the students' learning. I asked only that the boys stay a few minutes after class, right before they would be going home, to say a few *mizmorim* of *Tehillim* for me."

R' Dushnitzer stopped speaking, trying to decide how to phrase his next words without openly stating that his student had neglected to fulfill his request. At last, he continued, "But you know that this man is very busy doing many mitzvos. Apparently, being so busy and absorbed, he forgot to say *Tehillim* with his students. You are on your way to Yerushalayim now. Please, go see that principal and remind him of my request!"

R' Sholom asked, "Rebbe, how do you know he forgot?"

"Because I have not yet sold my orchard!"

Tremendously impressed by his Rebbe's faith in the power of prayer, R' Sholom set out for Jerusalem. On his arrival, he went at once to see his friend at the Talmud Torah. He found him rushing away to the post office, hoping to get there before closing time. R' Sholom reminded him of R' Dushnitzer's request. The principal confirmed their Rebbe's belief — he had indeed forgotten all about the request! Immediately he abandoned his other tasks, returned to the school, and said a few *perakim* of *Tehillim* with his students.

And — wonder of wonders — a week later, R' Eliyahu sold his orchard, paid off his debts, and was able to breathe easy again!

Panic!

וְכִחֶשׁ בָּהּ וְנִשְׁבַּע עַל שָׁקֶר
"And denied it and he swore falsely"
(Vayikra 5:22)

Two men came to R' Yosef Chaim of Baghdad, the "Ben Ish Chai," to resolve a dispute. One of the disputants had come to lodge a complaint against the other, who denied the charge.

They were in the midst of presenting the case when the Ben Ish Chai realized that the defendant was about to utter a false oath. Quickly, he said, "Did you think I was about to have you swear on a *sefer Torah?* Absolutely not! I intended to have you swear on the *Shnei Luchos HaBris* (Tablets of the Covenant)!"

Turning to his assistant, he ordered, "Go and bring the *Shnei Luchos HaBris!*"

Hearing this, the defendant was thrown into confusion. He had no idea that the Rav was referring to the *sefer* entitled *Shnei Luchos HaBris,* authored by R' Yeshayahu Horowitz — otherwise known as the Shelah HaKadosh. The defendant thought that the Ben Ish Chai meant the actual Tablets that Moshe Rabbeinu had brought down from Heaven. Being an ignorant man, he believed that the *Luchos* had gone along with the *B'nei Yisrael* when they were exiled.

In a panic, the man exclaimed, "I'll pay. I won't swear!"

"It's too late," the Ben Ish Chai replied soberly. "You have already obligated yourself to swear. Now you must follow through."

Even more frightened, the defendant admitted that he had lied, and that the other man's charges had been legitimate.

In All Fairness

וְהֵשִׁיב אֶת הַגְּזֵלָה אֲשֶׁר גָּזָל
"He shall return the robbed item that he robbed"

(Vayikra 5:23)

As a young man, R' Yaakov Lorberbaum, *av beis din* of Lisa and author of the *Nesivos HaMishpat*, once lent all his money to a wine merchant. The deal was made with a *heter iska*, as mandated by *halachah*. Through this transaction, R' Yaakov thought, he would be able to sit and learn Torah in peace while deriving an income from the wine merchant's profits.

One day, the merchant informed R' Yaakov that his business was floundering. Not wishing to cause R' Yaakov financial damage, the merchant was going to return the initial sum he had borrowed.

R' Yaakov accepted the money. Some time later, however, he learned that the same wine merchant had borrowed money from other people as well, but those investors had not received their money back. The wine merchant merely told them that he was going bankrupt and was unable to repay their investments.

Being a man who was known for his integrity in money matters, R' Yaakov was deeply pained by this information. *He* had received his share back, true — but what of the others? Would they lose everything they had invested?

R' Yaakov made up his mind. He went to the *beis din* and handed over the money he had received from the wine merchant, asking them to divide it properly among all the other investors. This left R' Yaakov himself all but destitute. Without money or a source of income, he was forced to accept a rabbinical position.

But he *was* left with one shining and supremely valuable asset: his noble and unwavering honesty.

Two men once came to see the holy R' Meir of Premishlan. They had formed a business partnership and wanted to receive his blessing for their mutual success.

"Have you already signed the partnership contract?" R' Meir asked.

"No, not yet," came the reply.

"In that case," said the *tzaddik*, "I will write the contract for you!"

Taking paper and pen in hand, he wrote the letters *alef, beis, gimmel,* and *dalet*.

"Here," he said, handing them the page. "Here is your contract."

The two men gazed at the letters on the paper, utterly bewildered. Seeing this, R' Meir explained.

"These four letters hold the secret of success for you. They form the initials of four crucial words. *Alef* is for '*emunah*' (faith). *Beis* is for '*berachah*' (blessing). *Gimmel* is for '*geneivah*' (stealing). And *dalet* is for '*dalus*' (poverty).

"If you conduct your business in honesty and good faith, blessings will crown the fruits of your labor. But if, Heaven forbid, you fall into dishonest practices and stealing — then poverty will surely follow."

꧁ ꧂

R' Moshe Alexanderov, a student in the yeshivah of Radin, used to help the Chofetz Chaim copy his handwritten manuscripts. It was decided between them that for every page of manuscript comprising a set number of lines, R' Moshe would be paid a certain amount of money.

Over some time, R' Moshe sat and copied manuscripts for his Rebbe, preparing them for the printing press. But one day, the Chofetz Chaim came to him in great distress.

"A catastrophe has occurred!" the Chofetz Chaim exclaimed. "I have been guilty of stealing!"

R' Moshe was stupefied. How could the Chofetz Chaim possibly have stolen? And what, exactly, was it that he was purported to have stolen?

The Chofetz Chaim explained. "When you started working for me, we agreed that you would be paid a certain sum in return for copying a specific number of lines on a manuscript page. But I have just learned that some of the pages had a greater number of lines than we agreed upon — lines that I never paid you for! Since it would be difficult to clarify the number of lines on each page, I don't even know the exact extent of my theft. What do I do?"

"Rebbe," answered R' Moshe, "I absolve you of paying it. I absolve you."

But the Chofetz Chaim did not want to hear that. He urged his student to accept more money, and would not budge from his position until R' Moshe agreed to accept the difference that the Chofetz Chaim had calculated he owed him.

In the courtyard of Petach Tikvah's Lomze Yeshivah stood two tall eucalyptus trees. The trees belonged to a man who lived near the yeshivah. When the holiday of Sukkos approached, neighborhood children would come — without asking the owner's permission — and snip branches off the trees to use as *s'chach*.

Seeing this, R' Eliyahu Dushnitzer would visit the trees' owner each year to purchase all the *s'chach* that the children had taken. Then he would "give" the *s'chach* to all those who had taken it, so that none of them would be guilty of sitting in a *sukkah* covered with stolen goods.

פרשת צו

Parashas Tzav

Do Not Delay

צַו אֶת אַהֲרֹן וְאֶת בָּנָיו לֵאמֹר

"Command Aharon and his sons, saying"

(Vayikra 6:2)

"'Command' can only be meant to express urging on, for the immediate moment, and for [future] generations." (Rashi)

A man once asked R' Yosef Chaim Sonnenfeld, Chief Rabbi of Yerushalayim, to speak with R' Mordechai Leib Rubin, the *Av Beis Din,* when next they met, to request his help in a certain matter. Both R' Rubin and this man lived in Jerusalem's Yemin Moshe neighborhood.

That night, a heavy snowfall enveloped the city. Standing at his window the next morning, the man saw a blanket of white covering the scene as far as the eye could see. Suddenly, he froze in his place. There, struggling to make his way through the snow, was none other than R' Yosef Chaim Sonnenfeld!

Anguished at having caused the elderly rabbi to face such hardship, the man ran out to meet him, weeping. He begged R' Yosef Chaim's forgiveness. "I never intended for you to make a special trip," he said tearfully, "and especially not in this kind of weather!"

R' Yosef Chaim was surprised. "Is it possible that an old Jew is forbidden to exert himself to do a *chesed*? After all, we learn not to delay when a mitzvah is at hand — and this principle applies equally well on snowy days!"

Too Late

צַו אֶת אַהֲרֹן וְאֶת בָּנָיו לֵאמֹר

"Command Aharon and his sons, saying"

(Vayikra 6:2)

"'Command' can only be meant to express urging on, for the immediate moment, and for [future] generations. [The Tanna] R' Shimon said: Scripture must especially urge in a situation where there is a loss of money." (Rashi)

As a young yeshivah student, the Chofetz Chaim was supposed to eat his main meal at a certain household one day. But his scheduled host changed his mind and, for various reasons, refused to feed the boy. It was explained to the man that this particular yeshivah student was truly exceptional, but not even this information made any difference: The man stood firm in his refusal. Young Yisrael Meir was left without a meal that day, and was forced to learn all day long while trying to ignore his hunger pangs.

Many years later, the two men chanced to meet. By this time, Yisrael Meir had become the illustrious Chofetz Chaim, respected even by the government authorities, and the other man had become a prosperous merchant.

The merchant had become embroiled in a legal dipute and had to stand trial. The danger of a lengthy prison sentence and a hefty fine hung over his head. In desperation, he turned to the Chofetz Chaim for his help in interceding with the authorities.

The Chofetz Chaim looked at him. "Do you remember that you once refused to take a hungry boy into your house to feed him a meal?"

Searching his memory, the merchant admitted that it was possible he had done so.

"That boy, who went hungry all that day, was me!"

The man paled. Shaken and afraid, he was shamed to the depths of his soul. But the Chofetz Chaim reassured him at once. "Nevertheless, I will fulfill your request, and do everything I can to help you!"

Deeply moved, the man said, "I am prepared to pay you anything you want — if only I can have a share in your Torah."

"You are too late," the Chofetz Chaim said. "Back then, you might have had a share, had you hosted me ... but not now. Today, you can acquire your share in Torah by supporting other hungry students in need of a meal!"

Efforts in Vain

צַו אֶת אַהֲרֹן וְאֶת בָּנָיו לֵאמֹר

"Command Aharon and his sons, saying"

(Vayikra 6:2)

"R' Shimon said: Scripture must especially urge in a situation where there is a loss of money." (Rashi)

It was the Fast of Esther. The Gaon, R' Eliyahu of Vilna, was traveling the roads in one of his periods of self-imposed exile. It grieved him that he might not be able to hear a public reading of Megillas Esther, since he was far from any Jewish community.

At last, spotting a laden wagon on the road, he flagged it down and asked the driver to take him to the nearest Jewish town, where he could hear the Megillah read in a shul. The wagon driver consented.

The Vilna Gaon climbed into the wagon and seated himself atop a pile of pots. The driver continued on his way.

Suddenly, the wagon swerved violently to avoid an obstacle in the road — and tipped over. The Gaon, sitting on top, fell off the wagon and was injured. The pots, too, rolled out and broke.

The driver was furious. To vent his anger, he began to rain blows on his bruised and bleeding passenger. He blamed the Vilna Gaon for not using his strength to keep the wagon from tilting onto its side and for causing the pots to break.

Hurt and aching, the Gaon escaped from the irate driver. The moment he was safe, however, his thoughts turned away from his injuries and he began to hurry toward the nearest town, anxious to reach it in time for the Megillah reading. But when he entered the town he found, to his dismay, that he was too late. The reading was over.

The Gaon tried to assemble ten men in order to read the Megillah in front of them, but was unsuccessful. He had no other option left but to pay ten men to form a *minyan*. He gave each of them two gold coins in advance.

Money in hand, the hired *minyan* was quick to betray him. As soon as he began to read the Megillah, they vanished. The Vilna Gaon was left alone. Despite all his efforts — efforts for which he had paid dearly, in blood and money — he had not succeeded in reading the Megillah with a *minyan*. He was forced to read it alone.

The Gaon felt distress over this for the rest of his life. He repeated this tale often, and whenever he did the tears would flow uncontrollably from his eyes.

In No Hurry

וְהָאֵשׁ עַל הַמִּזְבֵּחַ תּוּקַד בּוֹ לֹא תִכְבֶּה

"The fire on the Altar shall be kept burning on it, it shall not be extinguished"

(Vayikra 6:5)

On one of the trips he took in the course of his community service, R' Chaim Ozer Grodzinsky once spent Chanukah in the city of Cracow. While there, his coat tore and required mending. R' Chaim Ozer entered the home of a tailor — a simple man — just as night was falling, and requested that he repair the tear.

The tailor asked him to wait while he lit the Chanukah candles. Thinking that the tailor would be free within a few minutes, R' Chaim Ozer sat down to wait. But the tailor was in no hurry. He washed his hands, took off his work clothes, and put on his Shabbos finery. Then he lit the candles. Afterwards, he began to sing slowly, with great feeling and fervor, going through all the verses of *Maoz Tzur* and other songs of praise for upwards of half an hour. Only then was he free to mend R' Chaim Ozer's coat.

R' Chaim Ozer's reaction was enthusiastic: "I will never again be amazed at the way Cracow produces giants in Torah and piety. Just look at the preparations of a simple tailor and his joy at performing a mitzvah — so full of feeling and fire!"

During a discussion among the Kotzker Rebbe and his disciples, the subject of his brilliant son-in-law, author of the *Avnei Nezer,* came up. The Rebbe turned to his students and asked, "Do you know what the *Avnei Nezer's* father did to deserve such a son?

"It was Purim. Everywhere, Jews were busy and absorbed with the mitzvos of the day, feasting and drinking. R' Ze'ev Nachum thought, 'The whole world exists for the sake of the Torah. If everyone is busy with the mitzvos of Purim right now, what will become of the Torah?'

"Hurriedly he finished his *seudah,* went to the *beis midrash,* and sat and learned.

"A great commotion ensued in Heaven. With his Torah learning, R' Ze'ev Nachum maintained the world's existence in that hour. In this merit, he was worthy of having a son who would light up the world with his Torah and righteousness. And R' Ze'ev Nachum, who had no children up until then, was blessed with the *Avnei Nezer.*"

A *talmid chacham* who was very close to the Chazon Ish once came to him to hear words of encouragement and inspiration about learning Torah.

"Let me tell you a marvelous story about the Bach (*Bayis Chadash*) and the Taz (*Turei Zahav*)," said the Chazon Ish. "This is a story that illustrates the incredible value of learning Torah.

"The Taz was the Bach's son-in-law. When the match was being made between the Taz and the Bach's daughter, the Bach promised to support the Taz so that he might learn in peace, and he agreed to give his son-in-law meat to eat every day.

"It happened once that the Taz found a portion of lung on his plate instead of actual meat. The Taz summoned his father-in-law, the Bach, to a *din Torah,* claiming that lung was not meat!

"The *beis din* listened to both sides of the story, then ruled in favor of the *Bach,* concluding that the lung is also considered meat. The affair roused a great deal of astonishment. Why had the Taz brought his illustrious father-in-law to a *din Torah* over such a paltry matter?"

The Chazon Ish went on. "Do you know why the Taz did it? The Taz used to learn each day until he had used up the last drop of his strength. On the day that he ate the lung instead of meat, he had less strength than usual, and consequently learned a few minutes less than he normally did.

"This created a spirit of prosecution against the Bach up in Heaven. Because of the Bach, the Taz had learned a few minutes less than he might otherwise have done. The Taz, knowing this, summoned his father-in-law to a *din Torah* because he knew that the *beis din* would rule in favor of the Bach, as a lung is considered meat. And whatever is ruled down below is also the ruling up above. In this way, the accusation against his father-in-law would be dismissed."

R' Yisrael of Vizhnitz was once waiting for a train at the Turna station, when he turned to his assistant and said, "Meshulem, acquire the World to Come and bring me my *Gemara* so I can learn from it!"

"But, Rebbe," R' Meshulem protested, "the train is due to arrive in five minutes, and the *Gemara* is packed among a great many other things. It is hard to get to, and by the time I do, the train will have arrived."

"Meshulem, I am prepared to promise you whatever you want — just get me the *Gemara!* If you don't, someone will come to tell me a story, another will engage me in idle conversation, and the time will pass and be wasted."

R' Meshulem opened the bag, looked for, and found the *Gemara,* and handed it to the Rebbe, who began at once to learn with an expression of pure and holy pleasure on his face.

There was once a Jew who found it hard to fall asleep on *motza'ei Yom Kippur.* Seeing that sleep continued to elude him, he decided to use the time to learn. It was 3:30 a.m. when he made his way to the *beis midrash*. Imagine his surprise at finding the Vizhnitzer Rebbe, R' Yisrael, sitting and learning there — and this, after the holy and arduous labor of Yom Kippur!

The Sanzer Rebbe, R' Chaim, used to say that if someone is sitting and learning Torah, and a rifle is fired beside him, and he hears the noise, it is clear that he has not yet achieved a proper level of diligence in learning our holy Torah!

R' Chaim of Sanz was diligent both in the quantity of Torah that he learned, as well as the quality. His assistant, R' Raphael Seifer, once smelled smoke in the middle of the night. He hurried to the Rebbe's room. The Rebbe was standing by his table, his ailing foot up on a chair, studying a *sefer* lying at the table's edge. The candle had fallen over onto the table. The table began to burn — but the Rebbe noticed nothing.

R' Rapahel made haste to pour a bucketful of water over the flames. The Rebbe continued peacefully learning. He had noticed neither the flames, nor the water that extinguished them!

The Chofetz Chaim was once learning in a *beis midrash* when a fire broke out in one of the houses nearby. There was a very real danger that the conflagration would spread through the town. A great uproar followed, as young and old rushed to save what they could from the flames.

The fire was licking the *beis midrash* walls when someone suddenly noticed that the Chofetz Chaim was still sitting inside, absorbed in his learning and completely unaware of the imminent danger. In a flash they ran in, seized the Chofetz Chaim, and hurried him away from the scene of the fire.

"Why didn't you run out when you heard all the commotion?" the astonished townspeople asked him.

"I heard nothing," the Chofetz Chaim apologized with a smile. "Until you told me just now, I had no idea that anything was wrong."

So total was the *tzaddik's* concentration when learning Torah, that the flames were licking at his feet — and he neither sensed nor heard a thing!

A certain chassid and his son came to see the Sanzer Rebbe. The boy had just turned bar mitzvah, and his father wanted the Rebbe to bless him and ignite a spark of *yiras Shamayim* (fear of Heaven) in his young heart.

R' Chaim turned to the boy and asked him what he was learning. The bar mitzvah *bachur* began to discuss an argument between Rava and Abaye in the tractate *Bava Metzia*.

Enthusiastically, the Rebbe exclaimed, "Do you know, my son, who Abaye and Rava were? *Hakadosh Baruch Hu* took a torch of Heavenly fire, brought it down to earth — and that was Abaye. Then Hashem took another Heavenly torch and brought it to earth — and that was Rava!"

R' Yosef Shlomo Kahaneman related the following story, which took place during the period when he learned at the Chofetz Chaim's yeshivah in Radin.

One frigid winter morning, R' Kahaneman emerged from shul and learned that the Chofetz Chaim and his son-in-law, R' Tzvi, had just returned home after a difficult night's traveling. R' Kahaneman hurried off to greet them. First he went to R' Tzvi's house and welcomed him back, and then he went quickly to see the Chofetz Chaim. There, a surprise awaited him: He found the Chofetz Chaim sitting and learning the Rambam's *Yad HaChazakah* with deep concentration — so much so, that he did not even notice R' Kahaneman's entrance!

Not wishing to disturb his Rebbe, R' Kahaneman retraced his steps to R' Tzvi's house and related what he had just seen. But R' Tzvi was not surprised at all.

"All through our difficult journey over winding, ice-covered roads — a trip that took four long hours — the Chofetz Chaim never stopped learning for a moment," he declared.

That is true diligence!

A person close to the Imrei Emes, the Gerrer Rebbe, had this tale to tell.

"I once traveled with the Rebbe by train, and watched his every move all through the journey. I noticed that he did not stop learning Torah for even a minute.

"In the middle of the trip, there was a sudden jolt; the train had derailed. All the passengers climbed out of the cars and waited outside while the train was being fixed. As the others chatted among themselves and watched the progress of the repair work, the Rebbe went immediately to stand under a tree, pulled out his *sefer*, and continued learning without pause or break.

"The repairs took six hours. The workers brought heavy tools with which to get the train back on the tracks. All the other passengers followed their work with avid curiosity. The Rebbe did not lift his eyes from his *sefer*, but continued standing and learning in his place all through the long hours.

"When the job was completed and we were preparing to resume our journey, one young man who had been traveling with us approached the Rebbe and lightly touched his sleeve, without saying a word. The Rebbe returned to the train at once and climbed peacefully aboard, without a sign of weariness or exhaustion. There was no way that anyone could have known that he had just spent six hours on his feet in uninterrupted learning!"

A Burning Hunger for Torah

אֵשׁ תָּמִיד תּוּקַד עַל הַמִּזְבֵּחַ לֹא תִכְבֶּה

"A permanent fire shall remain aflame on the Altar; it shall not be extinguished."

(Vayikra 6:6)

R' Aharon of Klivan, one of the Ba'al Shem Tov's disciples, once came to the home of R' Ze'ev Wolf of Zitomir on the night known as "Nittelnacht," when the custom is to refrain from learning until midnight. Entering the house, he was greeted effusively by R' Ze'ev Wolf, who sat at the table with him and engaged him in a discussion. Afterwards, they ate the evening meal together. When they finished, R' Ze'ev showed his guest to a room with a bed laden with pillows and comforters, as befit such an honored guest. After R' Ze'ev went to his own room, R' Aharon began to approach his bed in order to rest on it — when he suddenly fainted.

The other chassidim tried to revive R' Aharon, but all their efforts proved futile. Afraid that the elderly man had succumbed to some sort of illness, they decided to knock on their Rebbe's door to tell him what had happened.

R' Ze'ev rushed to R' Aharon's room, seized his hands, and called, "R' Aharon, arise — it is midnight!"

In his wisdom and holiness, R' Ze'ev understood that his guest's fainting spell derived from no natural, physical source. Rather, R' Aharon was lacking some spiritual need. It was R' Aharon's habit to learn Torah day and night, and he knew numerous tractates of the Talmud by heart. It was most likely, R' Ze'ev believed, that R' Aharon had lost consciousness because he was unable to learn Torah during those hours. As long as he had sat together with R' Ze'ev and his host was fulfilling the mitzvah of *hachnasas orchim,* R' Aharon had remained strong. The moment he was left alone, however, his longing to learn became too powerful. Prevented from doing so by Jewish custom, his distress had become so great that he fainted.

As soon as R' Ze'ev's words reached his guest's ears, R' Aharon awoke at once. He washed his hands and began to review his *mishnayos* with tremendous pleasure and joy. All those present marveled at the wonderful sweetness with which the aged man reviewed the words of the beloved Torah.

Unknown Guilt

וְזֹאת תּוֹרַת הָאָשָׁם
"This is the teaching of the guilt-offering"

(Vayikra 7:1)

R' Moshe Avraham Galanti once came to the Ari Hakadosh and requested, "Rebbe, give me a *tikkun* for my *neshamah!"*

"I see no *tikkun* for your soul," the Ari soberly replied. "On your forehead I can clearly see that you have transgressed the prohibition, 'Do not delay paying your worker's salary'!"

The Ari's words shook R' Moshe Avraham profoundly. Plunged into the depths of misery, he left. Upon reaching his own home, he began to search through his actions, sobbing copiously all the while. He searched his memory in an effort to recall whom he might have harmed, whose salary he might have delayed paying — but to no avail. He could not remember.

R' Moshe Avraham owned a factory. He called together all his laborers and asked each one whether he had ever deprived him of what was rightfully his, Heaven forbid. It was only after a long and exhaustive inquiry that he finally learned that one of his workers had received two cents less than what was owed him for his labor.

R' Moshe Avraham paid the difference at once, then hurried back to see the Ari Hakadosh.

Smiling broadly, the Ari welcomed him with these words: "Your sin has departed and your transgression is atoned for!"

Gathering the Needy

וְאֵת כָּל הָעֵדָה הַקְהֵל

"Gather the entire assembly"

(Vayikra 8:3)

"This is one of the places [mentioned in Scripture] where the little held the many." (Rashi)

In the basement of the home of R' Yisrael of Vizhnitz was a kitchen where free meals were cooked for the needy. When the Vizhnitzer Rebbe moved to Grosverdein during the First World War, he continued his tradition of hospitality. Despite severe food shortages, when even his own family lacked proper nourishment, and despite the skyrocketing cost of foodstuffs, the Rebbe brought into his home hundreds of Jews who were fleeing the military authorities, and gave them room and board, free of charge.

Apart from these, many Jewish soldiers came to the Rebbe's home for a taste of kosher food. The Rebbe appointed a special *gabbai* to supervise the running of his kitchen. However, because he so loved the mitzvah of *hachnasas orchim,* welcoming guests, the Rebbe wanted to be personally involved in the mitzvah. His guests were once astounded to see the Rebbe enter the dining room carrying a tray laden with glasses of tea.

When they tried to take the heavy tray from him, he declined their help, saying, "Does it distress you to see me perform a mitzvah?"

One day, a Rav, who was also a relative of the Rebbe's, came to the house. When the Rav washed his hands before lunch, the Vizhnitzer Rebbe hurried to hand him a towel.

The Rav recoiled, refusing to take the towel from the Rebbe.

"But it's a *halachah* according to Beis Shammai!" protested the Rebbe. Seeing that his relative did not grasp his meaning, he added, "Beis Shammai rules that one is permitted to use a helper (*shamash*) who is an *am ha'aretz* (a simple, uneducated man)." [*Berachos* 52].

A Jew who, unfortunately, was distant from Torah and mitzvos once reached the city of Grosverdein by train in the middle of the night. Tired from his trip, the man longed to find a place to spend what was left of the night. He found a carriage for hire and made a deal with the driver: He was to search for an inn that was open. If he found none, the driver would take him back to the station.

The carriage plodded along the city streets for a long time, but the driver found no inn that was open, nor any house that was lit. They had almost given up when, in the distance, they saw a light shining from a window. The driver spurred his horses on in the direction of the light. A man, radiant of face, came out of the house to greet them and asked what they wanted. When the traveler explained his situation, the man invited him to stay in his home.

It was R' Yisrael, the Vizhnitzer Rebbe, who was up late learning Torah. Hearing the sound of the carriage's wheels rumbling outside his door, he had hurried out to greet his visitors. Now he invited the traveler inside and sat him at the table. Then he went into the kitchen and returned presently with a tasty meal for his guest. When the other man had finished eating, the Rebbe showed him to a comfortable bed. Wishing him a "Good night," the Rebbe left the room.

In the morning, the traveler woke from a refreshing sleep. Only then, to his amazement, did he learn the identity of his host, who had taken such pains to make him comfortable the night before. Upset,

the traveler approached the Rebbe to beg his forgiveness for having caused him so much trouble.

"I don't have enough money to pay his honor for the goodness he did to me!" the traveler said.

The Rebbe made little of his actions and tried to calm his guest. But the Jew was still in the grip of powerful emotions.

"Do you really wish to pay me for what I did for you?" the Rebbe finally asked. "You can repay your debt by improving your lifestyle and following the ways of the Torah!"

"I promise!" the man declared at once.

***

On another occasion, a young man from Tzefas found his way to the Rebbe's house. The young man's family had originally come from Vizhnitz. The Rebbe received him warmly and invited him to stay in his home.

Several days later, when the young man wished to take his leave, the Rebbe exclaimed, "But today is Shabbos! How will you travel?"

The young man was confused and distressed at hearing this, as the day was actually Wednesday. Noting his guest's confusion, the Rebbe explained himself.

"Today, in the *Shir Shel Yom* (Song of the Day), we recited the verse beginning *Lechu neranenah,* which we also say on Shabbos. And on Shabbos, we do not travel. Stay here with us and leave after Shabbos!"

The young man agreed to the Rebbe's request, and remained in his house for Shabbos.

On Sunday, when the guest again came to take his leave, the Rebbe gave him some money, saying, "This is for you and your family."

Then he gave the young man another respectable amount of money, adding, "This money is for *tzedakah*. Do not use it until you arrive in Eretz Yisrael. It will protect you on your journey, and you will arrive safely and without harm, for you are a *shaliach mitzvah* (messenger for the performance of a mitzvah)!"

Practice Makes Perfect

וַיַּעַשׂ אַהֲרֹן וּבָנָיו אֵת כָּל הַדְּבָרִים אֲשֶׁר צִוָּה ד' בְּיַד מֹשֶׁה

"Aharon and his sons carried out all the matters that Hashem commanded through Moshe."

(Vayikra 8:36)

"To tell their praise, that they veered neither right nor left [but did exactly as they were instructed]." (Rashi)

When he was 30 years old, R' Salman Mutzafi moved to Eretz Yisrael. He would *daven* in the shul of the *Chacham,* Tzadka Chutzin. Afterwards, the two would learn *Gemara* and the *Rishonim* together.

They came to the section of Tractate *Kiddushin* that discusses the laws of honoring one's parents. The Chacham Tzadka asked R' Salman, "When your mother passes you in the house, do you stand up for her?"

"Of course I do," R' Salman answered. "But not to my full height. I only lift myself up a little."

Immediately, the Chacham Tzadka closed his *Gemara.* "We will not continue learning today. It is impossible to learn something and not practice what one has learned. Standing up for one's parents means standing to one's full height. From now on, be careful to fully stand up for your mother. Only then will we be able to continue learning this *sugya!*"

The next day, R' Salman approached the Chacham Tzadka. "I've decided to perform the mitzvah of *kibbud av v'em,* honoring one's parents, as you have instructed me. I now stand up all the way for my mother."

The two then sat down and resumed their learning.

פרשת שמיני
Parashas Shemini

A Strange Gift

וַיֵּצְאוּ וַיְבָרְכוּ אֶת הָעָם

"And they went out and they blessed the people"

(Vayikra 9:23)

A young man received orders to appear before a military medical committee, which would determine if he was fit to serve in the army. In a panic, the young man ran to see R' Chaim of Sanz. The Sanzer Rebbe blessed him with success in avoiding military service, and gave him a box of cigarettes, "for the road." Though surprised at this strange gift, the young man dared not ask for an explanation. It was time for him to go.

It was near midnight when he arrived at the city where he was to have his examination the next morning. He entered an inn and sat down at a table. He was so exhausted that he fell asleep with his head on the table.

There were several other men seated around the large table. Two of them were playing chess while the others watched. As they concentrated intently on the game, all of them smoked continuously. They played and smoked — until the cigarettes ran out.

The men were at a loss. Smoking, they firmly believed, was an aid to concentration. To continue the complex game without cigarettes was impossible. But where could they find more cigarettes so late at night?

One of them pointed to the sleeping figure beside them. "Maybe he has some cigarettes."

They woke the young man, and asked, "Do you have any cigarettes?"

Yes, he had cigarettes — the ones the Rebbe had given him! He handed them to the players and went back to sleep. As for the others, their joy knew no bounds; they could now continue their game.

In the morning, the young man awoke, *davened,* and ate breakfast. Then, with a heavy heart, he made his way to his appointment. The doctors began to examine him, when suddenly, one of them exclaimed, "Hey! This is the guy who gave us those cigarettes last night, and saved our game!"

As a token of their appreciation, those chess-loving doctors signed a certificate exempting that young man from army service!

The Chofetz Chaim sat learning in the *beis midrash* one day, when a local blacksmith approached him, requesting a blessing for his sick daughter.

"I will do as you ask," the Chofetz Chaim said, "provided you give me ten rubles."

This astonished the blacksmith greatly, as he knew the Chofetz Chaim never took payment from anybody. However, he took ten rubles from his pocket and handed them over in return for the *tzaddik's* blessing for his daughter's speedy recovery.

Just a few days later, the daughter recovered from her illness. At the same time, the blacksmith's surprise over the Chofetz Chaim's request vanished when he received a letter from his son. This boy had left Radin, at the Chofetz Chaim's urging, to learn Torah in a distant yeshivah.

In his letter, the boy thanked his father for the ten rubles he had sent.

An uneducated Jew who made his living as a water-carrier decided one day that he wished to study the Torah. He went to R' Zalman Sender Shapiro and asked for a *berachah* to help him learn. R' Zalman Sender listened, and then said, "You are a water-carrier, healthy and strong. Scream out with all your might, three times: 'I want to learn how to learn!'"

The water-carrier, who was indeed healthy and strong, did as R' Zalman Sender told him. In a mighty voice, he roared out three times, "I WANT TO LEARN HOW TO LEARN!" By the third time, the walls were trembling. Then R' Zalman Sender blessed him that he would indeed know how to learn.

And, wonder of wonders, in a short time, that water-carrier, who had been ignorant and uneducated, achieved incredible levels in Torah learning and became an outstanding *talmid chacham*!

The Seeds of Greatness

וַיַּרְא כָּל הָעָם וַיָּרֹנּוּ וַיִּפְּלוּ עַל פְּנֵיהֶם

"*The people saw and sang glad song and fell upon their faces.*"

(*Vayikra* 9:24)

A resident of Tomashov who had known R' Menachem Mendel of Kotzk as a child was amazed at the fame that his childhood friend had garnered. "We learned together in *cheder*," he marveled. "How can it be that he's a Rebbe now?"

Hearing this, R' Menachem Mendel's chassidim began to question the man on the Rebbe's behavior as a child.

"I don't remember anything in particular about him," the man admitted. "He behaved like all the other children."

But the chassidim pressed him to try hard to remember if there had been anything special at all. And then the man recalled one incident:

"One Lag B'Omer, our *melamed* took us all on a trip to a mountain outside the town. We were surrounded by tall, majestic mountains. When teacher and students returned home, someone noticed that Menachem Mendel was missing. A search party went back to the mountain to look for him.

At the tip of the mountain, they found him lying on his back, arms and legs outspread. When they came close, they heard him murmuring the *pasuk*, '*Libi u'vesari yeranenu el Kel chai* — My heart and my flesh will rejoice in the living G-d.'"

He was not such an average child, after all.

R' Chaim and the Fire

וַיַּקְרִיבוּ לִפְנֵי ד' אֵשׁ זָרָה אֲשֶׁר לֹא צִוָּה אֹתָם

"And they brought before Hashem an alien fire that he had not commanded them."

(Vayikra 10:1)

When R' Chaim of Sanz was a small boy, a fire broke out in the city of Brody, where R' Chaim lived. The fire was large enough to force the family to flee to the neighboring city of Sassov. R' Chaim's mother took him — a boy not yet 3 years old — to see R' Moshe Leib Sassover. The boy had been very frightened by what had happened, and his mother asked the Rebbe to comfort him.

"Chaim," said the Rebbe, "tell me what you saw in that fire."

"On one side, I saw the Jews standing and putting out the fire," young Chaim answered, "and on the other side, I saw evil non-Jews who were standing and igniting the flames. It was hard for me to understand why we needed all that effort to set fires and put them out. Wouldn't it be better to just chase away the evil people who were setting the fires? Then there wouldn't be any flames to put out at all!"

A very powerful *mussar* message indeed!

An Early Seder

יַיִן וְשֵׁכָר אַל תֵּשְׁתְּ אַתָּה וּבָנֶיךָ אִתָּךְ בְּבֹאֲכֶם אֶל אֹהֶל מוֹעֵד

"Do not drink intoxicating wine, you and your sons with you, when you come to the Tent of Meeting"

(Vayikra 10:9)

It was Pesach night, and several residents of Jerusalem came to the home of R' Shmuel Salant at a fairly early hour, thinking that they would be able to observe the Rav in the middle of his *Seder*. To their surprise, they found R' Shmuel sitting over his *Gemara* and learning. His *Seder* was over and done with.

The visitors were unable to conceal their astonishment and they asked the Rav how he was able to finish the *Seder* so early.

"This has always been my custom," R' Shmuel replied.

And he went on to explain: "*Baruch Hashem,* Yerushalayim is a big city, and many people come to me with questions about *chametz* and matzah on this particular night. All the teachers, *dayanim,* and halachic authorities in the city are unable to rule tonight, as all of them drink four cups of wine at the *Seder* — and the *halachah* is that a drunk man may not instruct others. If so, to whom can the people come with their questions?

"I devised a solution to this dilemma. Each year, I finish my *Seder* quickly, and, immediately afterwards I sleep a little in order to dispel the effects of the four cups of wine that I drank. Then I am ready to rule and instruct anyone who comes to me with a question!"

The Case of the Switched Matzos

וַיִּקְצֹף עַל אֶלְעָזָר וְעַל אִיתָמָר בְּנֵי אַהֲרֹן הַנּוֹתָרִם

"And he was wrathful with Elazar and Itamar, Aharon's remaining sons"

(*Vayikra* 10:16)

Every *erev Pesach,* R' Yisrael of Vizhnitz would personally hand-bake three round matzos that he would use to perform the mitzvah. These matzos were carefully guarded until the *Seder* night.

One year, these matzos were accidentally mixed with the other matzos for the rest of the household. There was no way of distinguishing between one set and the other.

When R' Yisrael's mother heard about the mix-up, she grew angry at the servants for not being sufficiently vigilant. The news was then brought to the Rebbe himself. He calmed his household with the following story:

"In a certain *tzaddik's* house, special ingredients were prepared in the yard in honor of Pesach. Suddenly, one of the chickens got loose and jumped all over these items. A commotion arose, and a family member became furious with the servants for not properly supervising the food.

"Hearing the noise, the *tzaddik* ran out of his house and asked his relative, 'How is it possible that you are so angry?'

"'A *chametzdik* chicken has jumped onto the Pesach things!' the other justified himself.

"The *tzaddik* answered, 'Our Sages, may their memories be blessed, teach that a person who becomes angry is like one who worships idols — and you're telling me about a *chametzdik* chicken?!'"

Overcoming Anger

R' Mordechai of Neshchiz longed for a *tallis katan* that was made with material from Eretz Yisrael. His chassidim worked devotedly to obtain this for him, and finally succeeded in getting what the Rebbe wanted. One of his disciples approached the Rebbe and asked if he might please him by preparing the garment.

R' Mordechai gave him the material. The disciple tried his best, but he made a mistake and folded the garment twice — so that when it was cut, it had two neck holes!

The young man was terrified. How hard the chassidim had worked to obtain the fabric, how much effort they had put forth to get the precious material from Eretz Yisrael — and he had accidentally destroyed it. What should he do?

"How is the *tallis katan* coming along?" the Rebbe asked. "Is it ready?"

The poor young man stammered in fear, "Wh-what c-can I say? I made a m-mistake and cut two neck holes!"

He stood trembling, wondering how the Rebbe would rebuke him in his anger.

"Why are you afraid?" asked the Rebbe. "The garment really does need two neck holes. One for the usual purpose — and the other to test Mordechai to see if he'll get angry."

R' Yechiel Michel of Zlotchov was prepared to pay a fortune for an *esrog* — only he didn't have any money. He was destitute, and a good *esrog* was very expensive.

R' Yechiel Michel decided to sell his special *tefillin,* which had been bequeathed to him by his father, the Maggid of Drohowitz. There were many people eager to buy the illustrious *tefillin* and he made a quick sale. With the money, R' Yechiel Michel was able to buy a beautiful *esrog*. He carried it home, eyes glowing.

"Why are you so happy all of a sudden?" his wife asked. Poverty reigned in every corner of their home; there wasn't a spare penny to be found — but her husband was happy!

Carefully, R' Yechiel Michel removed the flax covering from the *esrog* and showed his wife the treasure he had acquired. The golden *esrog* shone as though to counter the terrible poverty. His wife looked at the *esrog* and then at her husband's radiant face.

"Where," she demanded, "did you get the money to buy this *esrog*?"

"I sold my *tefillin*."

"You sold the *tefillin* you inherited from your father? You sold the only valuable thing in this entire house — for an *esrog* that you'll use for seven days?" In a fury, she seized the *esrog* from her husband's hand, flicked off the *pitom,* and flung the *esrog* onto the floor.

R' Yechiel Michel surveyed the wreckage. Now he was minus an *esrog* and minus his precious *tefillin*. Raising his eyes to his wife, he said sadly, "I should get angry at you. But I have no *esrog* and no *tefillin* — and now the *yetzer hara* wants to trip me up with anger ... No. No, I won't do it."

That night, his father came to him in a dream and said, "My son, you sold my valuable *tefillin* in order to buy a top-quality *esrog*. This has made a great impression up in Heaven. But the second thing you did — your restraint in conquering your anger — has made an even bigger impression."

A young man came to R' Yitzchak of Vorka to complain about his father-in-law, who had reneged on his promise to support him a certain number of years so that he could learn Torah.

"Bring your father-in-law to me," R' Yitzchak said.

The father-in-law duly appeared, but all the Rebbe's gentle persuasion that he agree to help his son-in-law fell on deaf ears.

"This is not good," R' Yitzchak said. "I see that I will be forced to speak strongly, and that will lead me into the category of anger." At once, he ordered his assistant to bring him his Shabbos *kapote*. He reasoned: In this instance speaking angrily would be a mitzvah. But if he was going to embark on the mitzvah of speaking in anger, the mitzvah's honor deserved that he dress in his Shabbos finery!

Eating in Holiness

אָכוֹל תֹּאכְלוּ אֹתָהּ בַּקֹּדֶשׁ

"You should have eaten it in the Holy"

(*Vayikra* 10:18)

The daughter of the wealthy R' Yuzfa of Austria fell gravely ill. Her father distributed a great deal of money to the *talmidei chachamim* who learned in his *beis midrash,* so that they might pray for her recovery. Many of them also fasted on his daughter's behalf.

R' Yitzchak of Drohowitz was among those who learned in that *beis midrash.* When he received his share of the money, he promptly went home and made a large feast.

Later, when the girl had recovered, R' Yuzfa heard what R' Yitzchak had done and confronted him. "Is it possible?," he asked. All the others fasted — and you had a feast?"

"Had I fasted," R' Yitzchak replied, "it would have had little impact. Heaven is accustomed to my fasts. But when I threw a big feast, it made a large impression up in Heaven because I had changed my custom. My prayers were heard, and your daughter was restored to health."

Mysterious Behavior

אֶת זֶה תֹּאכְלוּ

"This may you eat"

(Vayikra 11:9*)*

In his youth, R' Yosef Zundel of Salant learned in the Volozhin Yeshivah, under the leadership of R' Chaim of Volozhin, a student of the Vilna Gaon. R' Chaim was very attached to his students, and he loved them all; but he loved R' Yosef Zundel more than all the rest and affectionately called him *"mein* Zundel" ("my Zundel"). Recognizing this prize student's greatness of spirit, R' Chaim would declare, "My Zundel is every inch a man!"

Early one morning, the other students saw R' Yosef Zundel walking through the non-Jewish section of Volozhin, with a pipe in his mouth. This scene repeated itself day after day, until the students began whispering amongst themselves about R' Yosef Zundel's strange behavior.

Their surprise was compounded by the fact that they knew R' Yosef Zundel's habit of old, which was to learn Torah from the earliest hour of the morning. Here, suddenly, was a whole new pattern: R' Yosef Zundel wandering the gentiles' streets early every morning — and with a pipe in his mouth, no less.

The news finally reached the *Rosh Yeshivah* himself. R' Chaim invited his beloved student to come and see him.

"*Mein* Zundel, they are saying that you walk the streets of the *goyim* every morning with a pipe in your mouth. Is this true?"

"Rebbe, it is true," R' Yosef Zundel answered humbly. "But there is a reason for my behavior.

"I heard that there are some Jews in Volozhin who buy bread from the *goyim.* Since such bread is forbidden, I decided to visit the non-Jewish bakeries every morning, where I ask permission to light my pipe from their ovens. At the same time, I throw a coal into the fire, which renders the bread no longer *pas nachri* (gentile bread). In this way, I save the Volozhiner Jews from eating something that is forbidden."

R' Chaim was extremely moved by his beloved student's concern for his fellow Jews, and blessed him: "May there be many more like you among our people!"

Breaking the Connection

וְנִטְמֵתֶם בָּם
"Lest you become contaminated through them"
(Vayikra 11:43)

R' Baruch of Mezibozh was once walking in shul on Shabbos when his *shtreimel* accidentally touched a light fixture that was hanging on the wall, moving it slightly to one side. Seeing this, R' Baruch was seized with fear and trembling, so much so that he fainted. It was only with difficulty that the others succeeded in returning him to consciousness.

"Why were you so upset?" they asked R' Baruch. "After all, the light was only moved slightly to one side, and it was not done on purpose."

"It wasn't the physical *aveirah* that distressed me," he answered, "as much as the knowledge that every sin a person commits pollutes his soul, as it says in the *pasuk*, 'Lest you become contaminated through them.' This contamination causes the light of higher understanding to be extinguished, and thus moves a person farther away from Hashem, in accordance with the severity of the sin. The greater and more holy a soul, the more a sin — even a small sin done involuntarily — causes the light of his *kedushah* to dim and his connection with Hashem to weaken, Heaven forbid.

"*That* is why I was so upset!"

A Bold Move

אַל תְּשַׁקְּצוּ אֶת נַפְשֹׁתֵיכֶם בְּכָל הַשֶּׁרֶץ הַשֹּׁרֵץ
"Do not make yourselves abominable by means of any creeping thing"
(Vayikra 11:43)

R' Shalom Kaski, one of the Torah leaders of Aram Tzovah, was a holy and pious man. It was said of him that he fulfilled everything that is written in the Kabbalistic *sefer* "*Reishis Chochmah*." R' Shalom's scrupulousness in performing mitzvos was legendary.

One *erev Pesach*, as he walked through the marketplace, he no-

ticed that there were bugs on many of the heads of lettuce for sale. He knew that most of the city's Jews would be ignorant of the proper way to check and clean the lettuce, and would transgress the serious prohibition against eating insects.

Without hesitation, R' Shalom bought up the contaminated merchandise, threw all the lettuce on the ground, and stamped on it with his feet — so that no Jew, Heaven forbid, would end up consuming a forbidden food.

The Anti-Bug Campaign

וְלֹא תְטַמְּאוּ אֶת נַפְשֹׁתֵיכֶם בְּכָל הַשֶּׁרֶץ הָרֹמֵשׂ עַל הָאָרֶץ

"And you shall not contaminate yourselves through any creeping thing that creeps on the earth."

(Vayikra 11:44)

R' Yehudah Tzadka's friends were frequent witnesses to the way Heaven protected the *tzaddik* from stumbling and committing even the smallest transgression. One *erev Pesach,* R' Yehudah Tzadka wanted all the lettuce which would be used for his *Seder* to be carefully checked for bugs. He announced that he would pay five *lirot* (a respectable sum in those times) for any insect found during the inspection.

After an exhaustive search, a neighbor of R' Yehudah's found a lone bug crawling around on a lettuce leaf. The neighbor refused to take the money, however, being glad that the merit of the mitzvah had come about through his hand.

But R' Yehudah insisted. He felt obligated to fulfill what he had said he would do, and pleaded with the man to take the money.

The Klausenberger Rebbe would describe the travails he suffered en route to Auschwitz. On his arrival at the camp, along with hordes of other Jews all herded together like sheep waiting to be shorn, there were long and tedious procedures to endure before any food was doled out to them. They had just endured three days of terrible conditions in the cattle cars, where many had died of hunger even before reaching the concentration camp.

At the sight of food, most of them pounced like starving animals. But the Klausenberger decided, "No matter what happens, I will not eat forbidden food!"

Many people advised him to change his mind, as this was a clear case of *pikuach nefesh* (a matter of life and death). But the Rebbe only *davened* to Hashem to save him from stumbling in this area.

As he waited in the long line for his portion of thin soup, a stranger came up to him and asked, "Is your name Halberstam? Are you a grandson of the Sanzer Rebbe?"

The Rebbe nodded, certain that the worst was about to happen. To break the Jews' spirit, the Nazis and their agents routinely sought out the rabbinical leaders and destroyed them.

The stranger, however, took a loaf of bread from beneath his coat, handed it to the Rebbe, and, with assurances that the bread was kosher, disappeared the way he had come.

The Klausenberger Rebbe took this as a sign from Heaven that his prayers had been heard, and that he would be able to survive the Holocaust without eating non-kosher food. And, indeed, throughout his long stay in the camps and despite periods of backbreaking labor, the Rebbe kept his promise to himself. At times, he was helped in this goal by Jews who were assigned to kitchen duty; at other times, people agreed to give some of their bread to him in return for his portion of soup.

At still other times, he simply chose to fast a day or even two, rather than let non-kosher food ever pass his lips.

The Correct Way to Answer a Poor Woman

זֹאת תּוֹרַת הַבְּהֵמָה וְהָעוֹף

"This is the law of the animal, the bird, etc."

(Vayikra 11:46)

It was the *Seder* night and R' Yechiel Michel Epstein had returned from shul. His family stood around the table, waiting to hear *Kiddush*. Suddenly, the door opened, and a woman entered with a question for R' Yechiel Michel about the *kashrus* of the dish she had cooked.

At first glance, it seemed that the food would have to be ruled not kosher — making both the food and the pot *treif*. But the Rav knew that the woman was very poor. Asking her to wait a moment, he went into the next room, where his *sefarim* were kept, and began to search through the halachic authorities among the *Rishonim* and the *Acharonim,* hoping to find something that would help the woman's case.

An hour passed, and still R' Yechiel Michel had not found a single ruling that would render the food kosher. Another hour went by as he continued to pore over his books. His family, growing tired of waiting, asked one of the grandsons, a boy of fourteen who was especially close to his grandfather, to go into the next room and ask his grandfather to come to the *Seder.*

The grandson went in to R' Yechiel Michel and said, "Grandfather, you are ruining our *simchas hachag* (the joy of our festival). If there is no way to make the dish permissible, then you must declare it forbidden."

"My dear grandson," R' Yechiel Michel answered, "you want me to finish up so that you will be happy on Pesach night — but that poor woman, should I declare her food non-kosher, will have her happiness ruined for the entire holiday!"

And again the Rav sat down. He kept searching until he finally discovered a way of rendering the dish permissible. He returned to the woman and told her that her food was kosher.

Only then did he sit down at the head of his table and share the holiday joy with his family.

Thanks for the Difference

לְהַבְדִּיל בֵּין הַטָּמֵא וּבֵין הַטָּהֹר
"To distinguish between the contaminated and the pure"
(Vayikra 11:47)

During the period when the brothers, R' Elimelech and R' Zusha, went through their self-imposed exile and wandered from town to town, they once spent the night at a certain inn. The innkeeper put them behind the oven in the main room. As R' Elimelech was the elder, R' Zusha always respectfully waited until his brother climbed into his bed before lying down on his own. On this night, therefore, R' Elimelech slept closer to the wall, while R' Zusha faced outward.

On this particular Monday night, the gentiles had gathered in the large front room to drink and make merry. As their intoxication grew, they began to sing and dance, swaying in the manner of drunkards. Suddenly, one of them noticed the two men lying on their pallets behind the stove. Nudging his companion, he said gleefully, "Let's get one of those Jews to amuse us!"

The idea found favor with the others. The men went behind the stove and pulled out the nearest Jew, who happened to be R' Zusha. They made him dance before them, and to help his feet move faster they poked his legs with sticks.

After he had been dancing for some time they threw him back behind the stove. Half an hour later, however, they hauled him out to dance for them again. When R' Zusha returned to his pallet the second time, R' Elimelech told him, "It is not right, my brother, that you should be made sport of by those gentiles while I lie here in peace. Let us switch places so you are lying closer to the wall and I am lying on the outside. When those men come seeking amusement again, they will take me, and you'll be able to rest!"

R' Zusha did not want to accede to this plan, but on his authority as the older brother, R' Elimelech insisted. They switched places.

But when the gentiles came a third time, they took "pity" on the Jew who lay on the outside. "This one's already danced for us. Let's switch dancers now — and take the one that's lying closer to the wall!"

And so, once again, the drunkards hauled R' Zusha to his weary feet and made him dance for them.

R' Zusha was overjoyed at the way things had turned out. Later, he said to his brother, "See? The one who is supposed to get the beating will get it. No plots or strategies will help."

At long last, the drunk men grew tired of their games. One by one, they fell to the ground in drunken stupors. There they slept off the effects of the night.

R' Elimelech rose from his pallet and joined his brother in a corner of the room to conduct their *tikkun chatzos*. And the two thanked Hashem from the bottom of their hearts for separating them from the gentiles and making their portion different from that of other nations, who drink and grow intoxicated and lose every semblance of their humanity — while we try all our lives to fulfill the Will of our Creator.

Perfect Clarity

וּבֵין הַחַיָּה הַנֶּאֱכֶלֶת וּבֵין הַחַיָּה אֲשֶׁר לֹא תֵאָכֵל

"Between the animal that may be eaten and the animal that may not be eaten."
(Vayikra 11:47)

The Gerrer Rebbe, author of the *Chiddushei HaRim,* had an amazing sensitivity to foods whose *kashrus* was suspect, even if strict *halachah* declared them permissible. The Rebbe was very strict with himself and did not eat any meat or chicken that was even slightly suspect, even if a Rav had declared the meat kosher.

One day, when the Rebbetzin was away from home, the new maid took a chicken to a Rav to ask if it was kosher. The Rav ruled that it was kosher, and the maid cooked it. Soon after, the *shamash* served the chicken to the Rebbe.

The Chiddushei HaRim took one look at the chicken and asked that it be removed from the table. The *shamash* went to the Rebbetzin and told her what had happened. The Rebbetzin, in turn, questioned the maid about the chicken, and heard that she had taken it to the Rav with a question about its *kashrus.*

The Rebbe, seeing the looks of astonishment on his family's faces at his remarkable sensitivity, said, "No doubt you are thinking that this is some special ability belonging to a Rebbe. It is no such thing. Every Jew can achieve a sensitivity like this! The Torah says, 'Between the animal that may be eaten' — that is, an animal that it is possible to eat — 'and the animal that may not be eaten' — that is, an animal that it is simply impossible to eat!

"This level of sensitivity may be reached in the following manner: If a person makes a firm and wholehearted resolution that, should something forbidden be found in his food or drink, he would rather choke upon it than eat it, then he will sense with perfect clarity whether the food is permissible, or not!"

ಒ๛

On one of the Ten Days of Repentance between Rosh Hashanah and Yom Kippur, R' Yosef Dov Soloveitchik, author of the *Beis HaLevi,* came to Brisk to visit his Rebbe, R' Yehoshua Leib Diskin.

As he prepared to take his leave at the visit's end, R' Yehoshua Leib told him, "You will still be on the road on *erev Yom Kippur.* I know you; you won't eat at anyone else's table. Therefore, I will supply you with half a cooked chicken for your *seudah hamafsekes,* the last meal before the fast."

R' Yosef Dov set out. When the time came for the *seudah hamafsekes,* his aide took out the chicken and served it to him. R' Yosef Dov looked at the chicken, smelled it, and said, "Something is not right here!" He pushed away the plate, with the chicken untouched.

When he reached his own home, R' Yosef Dov found a telegram waiting for him from his Rebbe, R' Yehoshua Leib. The telegram read, "There is a question regarding the chicken." (Of course, the question was a suspicion of a suspicion of a problem regarding a stringency, as was always the case with R' Yehoshua Leib.)

The next time R' Yosef Dov was in Brisk, he went to R' Yehoshua Leib to find out exactly what the question had been on that chicken. His Rebbe received him joyfully, embraced him, and recited the *berachah* of "*Shehecheyanu.*" Then he said, "I know that you did not eat from that chicken, as Hashem would not bring about a situation where a *tzaddik* such as R' Yosef Dov would stumble.

"In that case," he went on, "you must be wondering: Why did I send the telegram? I did so in order to fulfill the *halachah* that says that if a person discovers a question about the *kashrus* of a food, he must let others know.

"But I knew, all the same, that you had not eaten that chicken."

פרשת תזריע
Parashas Tazria

Horse Sense

אִשָּׁה כִּי תַזְרִיעַ וְיָלְדָה

"When a woman conceives and gives birth"

(Vayikra 12:2)

"The Amora R' Simlai said: 'Just as the fashioning of man [came] after all cattle, beasts, and fowl in [the Torah's account of] the act of Creation, so is his law explained after the law of cattle, beast and fowl.'" (Rashi)

A man came to the *tzaddik,* R' Meir of Premishlan, to lodge a complaint against another man whom he claimed was stealing his livelihood.

R' Meir replied, "You must certainly have noticed the way a horse, when drinking from the river, beats the water with its hooves. Perhaps you can explain to me why the horse behaves in this fashion?"

The man was stumped.

"As you know," the *tzaddik* explained, "water reflects like a mirror. As the horse bends its head to drink, he sees another horse in front of it, also drinking. This bothers the horse. Therefore, he beats at the water with its hooves, to send the 'other' horse away and keep the water all to himself.

"But you," R' Meir concluded, "understand that the river has enough water for many horses. In the same way, *Hakadosh Baruch Hu* can supply a livelihood for many people, and no one can touch what has been set aside for his fellow man."

Compassion

וּבַיּוֹם הַשְּׁמִינִי יִמּוֹל בְּשַׂר עָרְלָתוֹ
"On the eighth day, the flesh of his foreskin shall be circumcised."
(*Vayikra* 12:3)

R' Nosson Adler, Rebbe of the Chasam Sofer, was once invited to serve as *sandak* at a *bris* in a city quite distant from his own Frankfurt. Despite freezing cold and snowy weather, R' Nosson set out on his trip. He eventually reached his destination and was privileged to perform the mitzvah he had traveled far to fulfill.

After the *bris,* as the others were enjoying the meal, they suddenly noticed that R' Nosson was nowhere to be seen! An anxious search was instituted at once.

A little while later, R' Nosson was found at last, standing outside shaking from the cold. He was watching the horse and the wagon that had brought him there!

"What fault has the Rav found in my home," his host asked anxiously, "that compelled him to leave my warm house in order to wander around outside in the freezing cold?"

R' Nosson was quick to calm his host. Gently, he said, "I felt sorry for the wagon driver, who remained outside to guard his horse while we enjoyed the warmth of your home. I suggested to him that we switch places for a while. But a long time has passed, and he has not yet returned."

Members of the household went off in search of the driver. They found him sleeping peacefully beside the stove!

R' Nosson insisted that the driver not be woken. He was willing to return to the house — but only after someone else agreed to take his place at the horse's side.

The Gerrer Rebbe, author of the *Sfas Emes,* once asked a relative to take his two sons, Avraham Mordechai and Moshe Betzalel, to a certain Jew in Warsaw for a blessing.

The relative set out for Warsaw with the two boys. Upon his arrival, he began to seek out the Jew in question, assuming that he

was surely a well-known *tzaddik*. To his surprise, it took many long and exhaustive inquiries before he tracked the man down.

And, to his even greater astonishment, when he finally met the fellow he found him apparently nothing more than a simple Jew! He brought the boys and asked for a blessing, but the impression he received was that the man was equally bewildered by the request. Nevertheless, the Rebbe's relative was determined to fulfill his mission.

"Even if you know nothing about all this, please bless the children as their father, the Gerrer Rebbe, has requested," he said.

The man did so, placing his hands on the boys' heads and blessing them.

It was time to leave. The Rebbe's relative was still burning with curiosity to know who the man was and what he had done to merit such attention. Could he perhaps be one of the world's thirty-six hidden *tzaddikim?*

But there were no answers ... until he returned to Ger and heard them from the Rebbe himself.

"Yes, he is a simple Jew," the Rebbe said. "But once, when the time came to give his son a *bris,* he found that he had not even a penny to spend on a meal to honor the occasion. In order to raise money for a *seudas mitzvah,* he sold his bed linens. Afterwards, he was left truly destitute. This act, by a simple Jew, made a tremendous impression up in Heaven. It was decided to grant him a reward in this world as well — the reward that a blessing issuing from his mouth would find fulfillment.

"The man himself," the Rebbe added, "has no idea that he possesses the power to give blessings that come true."

Doubt

וְעָמֹק אֵין מַרְאֶהָ מִן הָעוֹר
"And its appearance is not deeper than the skin"
(Vayikra 13:4)

"I do not know its meaning." (Rashi)

A Rav once asked R' Yisrael, the Vizhnitzer Rebbe, about the source of a certain *halachah* in the *Choshen Mishpat,* and the Rebbe answered him.

"I think the Rebbe is mistaken," the Rav said respectfully. "I believe that the *halachah* is stated elsewhere."

But when he returned home and looked into the *Shulchan Aruch,* he discovered that the Rebbe had been correct. At once, he returned to the Rebbe to apologize, and expressed his regret at doubting him.

"I envy you," the Rebbe said.

"You envy me? Why?" the Rav asked in surprise.

"I envy you because you have nothing to regret except doubting my words."

R' Meir of Pesishcha once said, "When I was a boy and studied the *alef-beis* with my teacher, I learned an important lesson. I learned that when two people sit down and learn together, and each one negates himself before his friend and does not perceive himself as greater than the other — then *Hashem Yisbarach* forgives all their sins."

He went on to elaborate.

"I once asked my teacher, 'And what are these two dots?'

"'Those two *yuds* are the Holy One's Name.'

"When I saw two other dots, one on top of the other, at the end of a *pasuk,* I thought that they, too, formed Hashem's Name. But my teacher explained that if the two *yuds* are written side by side, with neither one higher than the other, that is Hashem's Name. But if you see two dots, like *yuds,* one on top of the other — that is not Hashem's Name.

"I learned from my teacher," R' Meir concluded, "that when two Jews sit together and neither one sees himself as greater than the other, they fall into the category of Hashem's Name."

The Shpoler Zeide would tell the following story, and he always began it this way:

"When I go up to Heaven and see the great locks on its gates, I will bring 'my thieves' with me to break open the locks and let all Jews' prayers ascend to the Throne of Glory."

Then he would go on to tell of a "holy thief," a man unique among all other thieves, known as Yossele the Thief:

"He had been a Jewish child, raised in a poor family, whose grandfather taught him Torah in his youth. Later, however, he strayed off the proper path and took up the distinctly unholy 'profession' of thievery.

"Despite his chosen profession, Yossele the Thief continued to identify himself as a Jew, and his grandfather would visit him and his cronies in jail, bringing them kosher food. At the end of his life, Yossele the Thief performed such a great *kiddush Hashem* that the adjective of 'Holy' was added to his name.

"He was once caught in the act of stealing from a church. The gentiles sentenced him to a torturous death: burning his body with boiling pitch. Then they offered him the option of saving himself by renouncing his religion and converting to their own. But Yossele the Thief shouted at the priests, 'I am a thief, but I am also a Jew. I will never abandon the faith of my fathers!'

"The priests dipped Yossele's hands in boiling tar and set it on fire. Yossele clapped his burning hands together and cried, 'I am a Jew, and I will die as a Jew!'

"The priests offered to heal his hands and promised him all manner of good things if he would agree to convert, but Yossele treated their offer with scorn. He embraced his suffering with love, and was burned to death *al kiddush Hashem*.

"He was buried in the Shpoler cemetery, and on his grave are carved the words, 'Here lies Yossele, the Holy Thief.'"

A Common Problem

נֶגַע צָרַעַת כִּי תִהְיֶה בְּאָדָם
"If a tzara'as affliction will be in a person"
(Vayikra 13:9)

When he was a boy of 7, R' Shmuel Salant fell ill. His parents sent for the doctor, who came to examine the child. In the course of the examination, the doctor asked Shmuel to open his mouth and show him his tongue.

The doctor turned to the parents. "This boy's tongue is not clean!"

Hearing this, young Shmuel responded instantly: "And whose tongue *is* clean? *Chazal* tell us [*Bava Basra* 165] that most of humanity engages in stealing, etc. — and all of them engage in some form of *lashon hara*!"

A man once went to the authorities to accuse the sons of R' Yisrael of Vizhnitz of evading the Romanian military draft. No one knew who the person was, though suspicion fell on one particular Jew.

That same week, this very man paid the Vizhnitzer Rebbe a visit. His chassidim expected the Rebbe to rebuke the man for what he had done, but the opposite happened. The Rebbe treated his visitor very warmly, and even served him a cup of wine.

One of the chassidim was unable to contain himself. With tears in his eyes, he asked the Rebbe, "How is it possible to treat that man warmly?"

"How do you know he was the one who brought the accusation?" the Rebbe countered.

"Everyone says he did it," the chassid replied.

"How can you accept *lashon hara*?" the Rebbe asked. "In order for the story to be believed, a court of three judges must be convened, and two witnesses must come forth to testify, as specified in the *Choshen Mishpat*. Only if this court rules against the defendant is it permissible to believe the charges laid against him. To merely rely on what 'people are saying' is absolutely forbidden!"

Tazria / 73

A Just Compensation

נֶגַע צָרַעַת כִּי תִהְיֶה בְּאָדָם וְהוּבָא אֶל הַכֹּהֵן

"If a tzara'as affliction will be in a person, he shall be brought to the Kohen."

(Vayikra 13:9)

R' Yechezkel of Shinova once came to visit his father, R' Chaim of Sanz. The two were sitting together, when a poor teacher came to the Sanzer Rebbe to complain of his difficult lot in life.

"I am about to marry off my daughter," he said, "and I don't even have enough money to buy the *chassan* a *tallis* and *shtreimel!*"

R' Yechezkel could not refrain from bursting out, "How can you say that? I saw you only yesterday, with my own eyes, in one of the shops — buying a *tallis* and a *shtreimel!*"

Greatly embarrassed, the man hung his head. Then, without a word, he got up and left.

As soon as he was gone, the Sanzer Rebbe turned to his son. "What have you done? You have humiliated a Jew for no reason. Perhaps he was only asking to see the *tallis* and *shtreimel* in order to judge their quality and see what they cost. And even if he actually bought them, as you say, he still needs money to buy his wife a new dress for their daughter's wedding. You have embarrassed an innocent man. You have no choice but to make your peace with him at once!"

R' Yechezkel ran after the man and begged his forgiveness. The man refused to forgive him unless R' Yechezkel agreed to come to a *din Torah* before his father, the Rebbe. R' Yechezkel agreed, and the man returned with him.

Before the teacher had even begun to lodge his complaint, the Rebbe said, "Do not forgive R' Yechezkel until he buys a *tallis* and *shtreimel* for your son-in-law, and pays all the wedding expenses."

R' Yechezkel happily complied with his father's ruling. He went at once with the poor man and bought the *tallis* and *shtreimel,* and then he provided enough money to pay for the entire wedding.

Changing Fortunes

בָּדָד יֵשֵׁב מִחוּץ לַמַּחֲנֶה מוֹשָׁבוֹ

"He shall stay in isolation; his dwelling shall be outside the camp."

(Vayikra 13:46)

"Our Rabbis have said: Why is [the one who suffers from tzara'as] different from others who are impure [that he should] stay in isolation? Since he caused a parting through malicious talk between a man and his wife and between a man and his colleague, he, too, shall be set apart." (Rashi)

Even when still in his youth, the Maharal of Prague was known throughout the city, and outside it as well, for his wisdom and outstanding Torah scholarship. From sunrise until the small hours of the night, he would sit in shul and pore diligently over the great collection of *sefarim* there.

R' Shmuel Reich, one of Prague's most illustrious citizens, wished to take the Maharal as his son-in-law, husband to his daughter, Perel. He promised to support the young couple and to remove all financial cares from the Maharal's shoulders. The engagement party was held amid vast joy.

Some time later, the Maharal received the following letter from his future father-in-law:

"A fire broke out in our town, burning whole neighborhoods to the ground, but did not touch the Jewish section. Because of this, the gentiles have accused us of setting the fire. A few days ago, they attacked my home and robbed it of everything they could lay their hands on. It pains me greatly to inform you that we are left with nothing. I will not be able to fulfill the commitment that I made upon your engagement, and am prepared to nullify the match."

"No no!" the Maharal decided. "Break the *shidduch* because of money? How could I distress a Jewish young woman that way?"

That very day, he dashed off an answer to his future father-in-law:

"I will not break off the *shidduch*," he wrote. "If, despite this, your honor wishes to break the *shidduch* anyway, let him first find another match for his daughter. Then I shall know what to do."

Years passed in which the Maharal continued to climb ever higher in Torah. For a part of that time he studied in the Maharshal's yeshivah, where his reputation spread far and wide as a *gaon* who was well versed in the entire Torah.

Meanwhile, in his prospective father-in-law's home, the struggle for a livelihood continued. Perel and her mother did their share to help earn the family's living: The mother baked bread and cakes and the daughter sold them in a small shop near their home.

One day, Perel laid some freshly-baked loaves of bread on the windowsill of the shop. A hungry officer, passing by, found the fragrance irresistible. He drew his sword, thrust it into one of the loaves, picked it up, and began to eat it.

Perel ran out of the shop. Seizing the reigns of the officer's horse, she began to scold him for stealing her poor parents' meager livelihood.

"Believe me," the officer assured her, "I have just returned from the battlefield and have not tasted a morsel for three days. What would you have me do? I don't have as much as a penny in my pocket to pay for the bread."

Perel stood where she was, her eyes filling with tears. The soldier's heart softened. Handing her a saddle, he said, "Here, take this as a guarantee of payment. I found this saddle and took it, but I don't really need it. If I do not return within two days, let the saddle be your payment!"

Perel took the saddle, and the officer mounted his horse and trotted away.

The two days passed, and then a few weeks, without a sign of the soldier. Perel picked up the saddle, which had been lying in a corner of the shop, and examined it more closely. To her amazement, she found gold coins sewn into the lining!

"Mother, Father!" she cried joyously. "Look what I found in the saddle! Many gold coins — a gift from Heaven!"

Her parents, hurrying over, could hardly believe their eyes.

At once, they remembered their beloved, prospective son-in-law, still learning in yeshivah and growing ever greater in Torah. The Maharal had not married anyone else. In short order, Perel's father sent off a letter in which he renewed his commitment to support the Maharal and his wife, and requested his agreement.

The day the Maharal received the letter was one of unbounded joy. The wedding was held in Prague amid great exultation, and was enthusiastically celebrated by the city's entire Jewish population.

Tazria / 77

It was R' Yitzchak Blazer's custom to accept any invitation to a *simchah* without any consideration as to whether the invitation accorded well with his own honor. In R' Yitzchak's opinion, this policy fell into the category of *gemilus chassadim,* performing kind deeds.

There were occasions when this custom aroused considerable astonishment.

Rebbetzin Meltzer related the following incident.

In a town near Kovno, an ignorant youth — a plasterer by profession — decided one day that he wished to study Torah. He went to the local shul and remained there, learning without cease, while righteous Jewish housewives brought him food to sustain him. Slowly, he taught himself *Chumash* until he had begun to attain some understanding of it.

Eventually, the youth became engaged to be married. The wedding was celebrated in another city, and R' Yitzchak made a special trip to attend it. Seeing him there, the city's Rav was astounded. "Why," he asked, "did his honor see fit to travel to attend this wedding?"

"It falls into the category of *gemilus chassadim,*" R' Yitzchak replied. "We cannot overestimate the merit of an act of kindness!"

Upon his return home, R' Yitzchak learned that a near-tragedy had occurred while he had been away. One of his children had swallowed a coin, which had become stuck in his throat. Kovno's physicians had worked feverishly to either extract the coin or to induce the child to swallow it. Their efforts were all in vain.

Suddenly, in a manner not at all in accordance with natural law, the boy swallowed the coin on his own and emerged unharmed from the incident. In R' Yitzchak's opinion, this miraculous rescue had occurred in the merit of the *chesed* that he had just done.

When attending a wedding, R' Yitzchak did not satisfy himself with supplying his mere presence at the affair. He was the life and soul of the party. Standing on a table, he would sing and dance, compose rhymes, and perform all sorts of antics for the bride and groom's pleasure. The people cherished their many happy memories of the way R' Yitzchak threw himself into each and every *simchah.*

At the second marriage of his friend, R' Naftali Amsterdam, both men were over 70. At the wedding, R' Yitzchak behaved no differently than usual. He danced and sang and did all he could to gladden the couple's hearts. Asked the reason for this, R' Yitzchak said simply, "When it comes to the imperative of bringing joy to a *chasan* and *kallah,* there is no difference between an 18-year-old and someone who is 70!"

A new student arrived at the Kelm Yeshivah. Young and unsure of himself, he entered the yeshivah building hesitantly and took a few steps down the corridor. There he encountered one of the yeshivah students.

"Hello!" the older student exclaimed. "How are you?"

The new boy answered with restraint, but the other student persisted. Warmly, he asked a series of interested questions. "What time did you arrive? Do you have a place to sleep? A place to eat?"

To hear him, you would have thought the older student was one of the new boy's oldest friends. In fact, that was exactly what the new student thought.

"But who is he?" the new boy asked himself. "Why doesn't he tell me his name? His face must have changed; that's why I don't recognize him."

A moment later, another boy appeared on the scene. He, too, approached the new student.

"Hello!" he exclaimed, like an old friend. And once again, the new boy was inundated with warm and interested questions concerning his welfare.

"He must also be one of my old friends," the new boy thought. "But I don't recognize him, either!"

It was only after nearly all the other students he met greeted him in the same warm and heartfelt manner that he understood — such behavior was typical of this place.

Indeed, an attitude of friendliness toward one's fellow man was prominent in Kelm. The yeshivah's students trained themselves in various ways, one of which was to welcome all newcomers with great warmth. Any student who happened to cross the newcomer's path would approach him with a hand outstretched to greet him and a friendly interest in his welfare.

When the month of Elul came around and it was time to look inward and do *teshuvah,* the *Rosh Yeshivah,* R' Simchah Zissel Ziv, would hang up an important announcement on the yeshivah wall. The subject: love for one's fellow man.

On Rosh Hashanah, the entire student body resolved to greet all people *b'seiver panim yafos,* warmly and graciously. They knew that this is the time of year when people, trembling and afraid, walk around with sober faces and preoccupied manners. It is not a time when people pay much attention to their fellow men. Therefore, the students of Kelm found it fitting to undertake this resolution specifically on the Day of Judgment: to relate to all people in a spirit of friendliness, and to greet them with faces that were radiant and joyous.

R' Moshe Feinstein and a guest were eating breakfast one morning. Towards the end of the meal, when the coffee was served, two containers of milk were placed on the table. Both were from companies known for their strict *kashrus.* R' Moshe picked up one container and then as though changing his mind put it back and took the second one.

The guest jumped to the instant conclusion that R' Moshe would not completely rely on the first company's standard of *kashrus* and preferred that of the second. He decided to spread the word to others who were scrupulous about their own standards of *kashrus.*

The news took flight. Many stopped buying the first company's products to the point that shopkeepers who had been purchasing from that company stopped doing business with them. Understandably distressed, the company's owners paid R' Moshe a visit.

"What flaw have you found in the *kashrus* of our products?" they asked.

"No flaw at all," replied R' Moshe. "In fact, I drink your milk." And to prove it, he opened his refrigerator to show them the containers of their milk inside!

The owners then raised the question that was uppermost in their mind, asking about that breakfast where R' Moshe had apparently changed his mind and reached for the second container of milk.

R' Moshe smiled. "There is a simple explanation. The first container was empty. There was no milk left inside."

פרשת מצורע

Parashas Metzora

"Stop the Coach!"

וְצִוָּה הַכֹּהֵן וְלָקַח לַמִּטַּהֵר שְׁתֵּי צִפֳּרִים חַיּוֹת טְהֹרוֹת

"The Kohen shall command; and for the person being purified there shall be taken two live, pure birds"

(Vayikra 14:4)

"Pure to the exclusion of an impure fowl, [i.e. a fowl of a non-kosher species]. Since afflictions [of tzara'as] come about because of malicious talk, which is an act of verbal twittering, therefore, there was required for [the sufferer's] purification, birds that constantly twitter with [the] chirping of sound." (Rashi)

The Chofetz Chaim once traveled in a coach together with several horse and cattle merchants. Along the way, the merchants were discussing their trade. The Chofetz Chaim, absorbed in his own thoughts, paid no attention to their talk.

All at once, one of his fellow passengers brought up the names of their competitors, and the merchants began to make fun of them.

As though waking from sleep, the Chofetz Chaim sat up and admonished them in a pleasant tone. "My brothers! Until now, you have engaged in a nice conversation about horses and cattle, your source of livelihood. Why have you moved on to talk about people? That brings with it grave transgressions of *lashon hara* (malicious talk) and *rechilus* (slander)!"

The other passengers, simple people, had no idea who was addressing them. They treated his admonition with scorn. "Stay out of our affairs! Who are you to give us *mussar*?"

R' Yisrael Meir did not respond to their abuse. On the contrary, he was pleased that this turn in the conversation prevented them from speaking *lashon hara*. But when they had finished their diatribe against the Chofetz Chaim, the merchants picked up the thread of their interrupted discussion. Once again, the Chofetz Chaim rebuked them, and begged them to go back to cattle and horses.

Finally, seeing that his words had no effect, the Chofetz Chaim called to the driver to stop and let him out. He preferred to be stranded in the middle of the road than to sit in a gathering of frivolous men engaged in speaking *lashon hara*!

In the course of one of his trips to sell his *sefer*, the Chofetz Chaim ended up spending a Shabbos in a certain town, as the guest of a *shochet*.

As he was preparing to wash his hands before eating the third Shabbos meal, the Chofetz Chaim overhead the *shochet* telling his wife that Yosef the butcher had tricked a certain individual, telling him that the meat that had been slaughtered the previous day was *glatt*.

The Chofetz Chaim left the house immediately, without a word.

When the *shochet* noticed his guest's absence, he began scouring the town for him. He found the Chofetz Chaim at last, eating the meal at someone else's house.

"Why did you leave my house so suddenly?" the *shochet* asked.

"I cannot stay there anymore," the Chofetz Chaim replied. "If you have a complaint against the butcher, that's a halachic issue that should be brought to the Rav's attention. Alternatively, you could rebuke him privately. But how do you come to tell the story to your wife? It's *lashon hara*!

"Here I am, selling *sefarim* that teach caution in staying far from forbidden speech. How can I remain as a guest in a home where *lashon hara* is spoken?"

Humble Silence

וּשְׁנִי תוֹלַעַת וְאֵזוֹב

"Crimson thread and hyssop"

(*Vayikra* 14:4)

"What is his remedy that he should be cured? He should lower himself from his arrogance like a worm and like hyssop." (Rashi)

In the city of Petersburg, there was a gathering of *gedolei Yisrael*. Among those participating in the meeting was R' Yosef Dov

Soloveitchik, the Brisker Rav. In the midst of the gathering, R' Yosef Dov presented a complex and difficult Torah question in the name of his son, R' Chaim. An interesting and avid discussion about this question took place, each Rav presenting his own thoughts and responses to the query.

Only one man did not partake in the conversation. Throughout the whole discussion, Rav Yitzchak Blazer sat quietly and did not offer any of his thoughts on the matter.

In the end, R' Yosef Dov put forth an answer of his, as well as one that his son, R' Chaim, had offered. All those who had been involved in the discussion nodded in assent and accepted R' Yosef Dov's answers.

R' Yosef Dov was very surprised at the silence of R' Yitzchak Blazer. "And they say that he is a great man?" he wondered to himself.

When R' Yosef Dov returned home, he immediately requested that the *sefer* that R' Yitzchak had authored, the *Pri Yitzchak*, be brought to him. To his incredulity, he found that R' Yitzchak had asked the exact same question that he had asked at the assembly. And furthermore, R' Yitzchak had answered the question with the two identical answers: that of R' Yosef Dov and that of his son, R' Chaim!

R' Yosef Dov was amazed at the incredible restraint of R' Yitzchak, and exclaimed, "How great is the humility of R' Yitzchak Blazer, who was able to listen to the Torah debate in silence for hours, without saying a word, although he had the answers all along!"

When the Chofetz Chaim brought his *sefer* to R' Baruch Mordechai Lifshitz, one of his generation's *geonim,* for a *haskamah* (approbation), R' Lifshitz became very excited over what he read. Nevertheless, he did not want to grant his approbation before he ascertained that the author of the *sefer* was a man who lived up to its contents.

He began to ask various *talmidei chachamim* to speak to the author, R' Yisrael Meir, on Torah and other topics. In the course of these conversations, they were to introduce the names of Jews who were known to have said damaging things about Judaism. He wanted to see how the author of the *sefer* observed the *halachos* of *lashon hara*.

One of the Torah scholars asked to perform this test was R' Nosson Nata. Again and again, he tried to trip up the Chofetz Chaim, to extract at least one piece of *lashon hara* from his lips. But not even the tiniest tidbit came out of his mouth.

Only then did R' Lifshitz agree, with a full heart, to give the *sefer* his *haskamah*.

✦

The holy *tzaddik* of Pesishcha once instructed R' Simchah Bunim to travel from town to town but did not reveal the purpose of the mission. R' Simchah Bunim took several chassidim with him and together they set out. They arrived at a certain village, and asked one of the householders if they might eat at his table.

"You are welcome to eat with me," the man said. "But I have no dairy food in the house at present, only meat."

The chassidim launched an extensive inquiry into the meat in question. Who was the *shochet*? Was the animal kosher and unblemished? Had the salting and rinsing been performed according to *halachah*?

They were still asking their questions when a new voice spoke up. It came from a man in tattered clothes, seated behind the stove. He looked like one of the many poor folk who traveled from town to town.

"Chassidim, chassidim! You spend so much energy investigating what goes into your mouth! But concerning what *leaves* the mouth — a person's speech — you ask not a single question."

Hearing this, R' Simchah Bunim decided that it was to hear this piece of wisdom that the holy Rebbe had sent him here. With that, he turned around and went right back home again.

No Atonement

וְעֵץ אֶרֶז
"And cedarwood"
(Vayikra 14:4)
"Because afflictions [of tzara'as] come because of haughtiness"
(Rashi)

R' Chaim Elazar Wachs, Rav of Kalisch, was in the midst of delivering a *shiur* to his students when a stranger walked in. The man broke into the thread of the Rav's thoughts, offering his own, not very valuable, insights instead. R' Chaim Elazar listened attentively to the stranger, who shortly began to spout such fanciful reasoning that the other members of the *shiur* could not hold themselves back from laughing out loud.

R' Chaim Elazar apologized at once on his students' behalf, and even went so far as to invite the man to come again some other time. Soon afterwards, the stranger left.

Agitated, the Rav took to his feet and ran after the man until he caught up with him. They stood deep in conversation for several moments.

When R' Chaim Elazar returned, his students expressed their surprise. "Why did the Rav react that way?"

"My sons," exclaimed R' Chaim Elazar, "you nearly lost your portion in the World to Come! You transgressed the serious prohibition of embarrassing another person! I ran after him to beg his pardon on your behalf, and went on working to extract every grudge from his heart, until I knew that he forgave you completely.

"But from now on," the Rav concluded, "be very careful with other people's honor because, for this sin, there is no atonement."

The Ba'al Shem Tov once appointed R' Ze'ev Wolf Kitzes to be the *ba'al tokei'a* (shofar blower) in his shul, and offered to teach him the hidden meaning and significance of each *teki'ah* (blast of the shofar). R' Ze'ev Wolf, afraid that he would forget something, wrote everything he learned on a piece of paper to keep with him as a reminder.

When the time came for him to blow the shofar, however, he found that he had lost the paper. This discovery distressed R' Ze'ev Wolf so much that he broke into heartbroken sobs. Still sobbing, he blew the shofar.

Afterwards, the Ba'al Shem Tov asked him if he had borne in mind the intentions he had taught him. Sadly, R' Ze'ev Wolf admitted that he had lost the paper on which he had written everything, and had been forced to blow the shofar in a brokenhearted state.

The Ba'al Shem Tov laughed. "This time, the *teki'os* went up correctly," he said. "There are many chambers in the King's palace, and the various intentions are like keys that open the doors of those chambers. If you forget one intention, you are unable to open one door. But there is one special key that opens all the doors and gates, and that is the key of heartbreak.

"Today, you opened all the doors."

A certain tailor, who lived near Pesishcha, was much patronized by the local *poritzim* (noblemen). One *poritz* bought material with which to fashion a coat. Summoning the tailor, he said, "This fabric is very expensive. Try to make a coat suited to the material."

With a laugh, the tailor said, "Why do you bother telling me this, sir? Aren't I the most expert tailor in these parts?"

The *poritz* gave the tailor the material, and the tailor made the coat. When he brought back the finished product, the *poritz* tried it on to see whether it fit. In the *poritz's* opinion, it didn't. He and his men began to berate the tailor for ruining the coat, and ended by throwing him out of the house and tossing the coat out after him.

This incident caused the tailor to lose a great deal of business. He was soon without a source of livelihood. His wife said, "Everyone goes to see R' Yerachmiel, son of the holy *tzaddik* of Pesishcha. Listen to my advice and go to him also."

The tailor went to see R' Yerachmiel, and sadly poured out his story.

"Take out all the stitches in the coat," R' Yerachmiel advised, "and sew it again using the same stitches. Then bring the coat back to the *poritz*."

The advice seemed absurd to the tailor, but for lack of any alternative he decided to take it. When he brought along the newly sewn coat, it found great favor in the *poritz's* eyes! The *poritz* summoned his wife to see how well he looked in the coat, and they both showered the tailor with praise as well as with a hefty bonus.

Later, the tailor returned to R' Yerachmiel to tell him what had happened.

"I realized that you had sewn the first coat with arrogance and pride," the *tzaddik* explained. "And since arrogance has no quality of pleasing, the coat did not find favor in your customer's eyes. When you came to see me, however, I saw that you were feeling humble and low. That's why I suggested that you undo the stitches of pride and sew the coat again. This time you sewed the coat with humility.

"The new coat, as you saw, was pleasing in the extreme."

From time to time, R' Moshe Leib of Sassov would visit the marketplace. Once, on his arrival, he found the marketplace empty. A troupe of acrobats had come to perform, attracting the entire crowd.

The animals were left without food or drink. Thirsty and discouraged, they lowered their heads weakly. R' Moshe Leib took a pail of water and passed among the beasts, slaking their thirst, and his own joy knew no bounds.

One of the merchants, passing by, remembered that his own animals had not been watered. "Hey, water carrier!" he called to R' Moshe Leib, "while you're at it, give some to my animals, too. They're standing over there, in that alley to the left. Hurry!"

R' Moshe Leib nodded his head in assent, and immediately hurried into the alley on the left to water the merchant's animals.

R' Zusha Triumphs

וְצִוָּה הַכֹּהֵן וְלָקַח לַמִּטַּהֵר שְׁתֵּי צִפֳּרִים חַיּוֹת טְהֹרוֹת
וְעֵץ אֶרֶז וּשְׁנִי תוֹלַעַת וְאֵזֹב

"The Kohen shall command; and for the person being purified there shall be taken two live, pure birds, cedarwood, crimson thread, and hyssop."

(Vayikra 14:4)

"Crimson thread and hyssop. What is his remedy [i.e., what is the remedy of one who is guilty of malicious talk or haughtiness], that he should be cured [of his affliction]? He should lower himself from his arrogance like a worm and like hyssop. (Rashi)

R' Zusha of Anipoli was forever fleeing honor. He lived in extreme poverty, so that when his daughter reached marriageable age he did not have even a penny with which to marry her off. Still, he trusted in his Creator. Hashem would surely not abandon him in his hour of need.

One day, R' Zusha was summoned to the home of his Rebbe, the Maggid of Mezritch. R' Zusha immediately traveled to Mezritch, and when he entered his Rebbe's room, the Maggid said, without preamble, "I know, Zusha, that you have no money with which to marry off your daughter. Here are 500 rubles. Go home at once, and Heaven will help you find your daughter her proper match!"

R' Zusha set out for home. As he passed through a certain town, he noticed a commotion in a shul courtyard. Drawing closer to learn the cause of the disturbance, he saw a *chuppah* standing ready in the courtyard. Beside it stood the bride and her mother, both weeping bitterly.

R' Zusha quickly learned the story. The mother of the bride, a widow, had painstakingly saved up her money, penny by penny, in order to marry off her daughter. And now, the money was gone! The *chasan* and his family had declared, in no uncertain terms, that until the dowry money was in their hands, a sum of 500 rubles, there would be no wedding.

R' Zusha went over to the *kallah's* family. "I found a bundle of money, but I must hear a description from you. What kind of bills were there? How was the money wrapped?"

The distraught widow answered his questions.

"Yes, that's the money I found," R' Zusha said. "Wait here and I'll bring it!"

The widow showered him with blessings and thanks, as did the bride and the entire family, "May this upright and compassionate man be blessed. He is a messenger from Heaven, sent to avoid shaming a Jewish bride."

Only minutes passed before R' Zusha returned, carrying a bundle of money that exactly matched the widow's description. Then, to everyone's surprise, he said, "I get 10 percent of the money."

A shocked silence reigned for a moment. Then the bride's uncle cried, "The nerve! Returning something to its owner is a mitzvah from the Torah and he's asking for a commission!"

"How can you hold up your head? Aren't you ashamed of yourself?" fumed the bride's mother. "Can't you find some compassion in your heart for a poor Jewish bride?"

But R' Zusha was adamant. Either he received 10 percent of the money, or he would not give it back.

Now the *chasan's* family joined forces with the *kallah's* in shouting at and abusing R' Zusha. The altercation reached the point where actual fists were raised.

"Let's go to the Rav!" someone called. The crowd marched off to see the Rav, dragging R' Zusha along with them.

After hearing both sides, the Rav naturally ruled that R' Zusha was obligated to return the entire sum of money to the widow. R' Zusha was sent away from the town in humiliation, and the bride was married with honor, knowing that the lost money belonged rightfully to her mother.

Days passed, and then weeks. The Maggid of Mezritch happened by that same town, and heard the story of the poor-looking traveler, with the appearance of a chassid, who had found the widow's money. The Maggid understood that the traveler was none other than R' Zusha. Later, he asked for an explanation of his disciple's strange behavior.

"When I saw that orphaned bride and her mother standing and crying, I was overcome with pity and decided at once to give them the money. But as I stood in line at the moneychanger's to change the bills, the *yetzer hara* (evil inclination) began whispering in my ear: 'You are a *tzaddik,* an incredible *tzaddik!* Choosing to help another Jewish daughter over your own. Yes, yes, you are greater than Avraham Avinu!'

"So I told my *yetzer*, 'Aha, you are trying to trip me up with arrogance! That won't do! You'll see — I'll make them take the money from me by force, and send me away with curses, covered with shame!'

"And that," R' Zusha concluded with a smile, "is exactly what I did."

The residents of Brody, home of R' Ephraim Zalman Margalios, began to notice something strange. Every morning, when R' Ephraim Zalman made his way to shul for *Shacharis,* he would not take the most direct route. Instead, he would lengthen the walk by two extra blocks.

"How strange!" the people said. "Why would he walk down those two blocks? He could save himself precious time by avoiding them altogether! He's always so careful about time, using every minute to learn Torah."

Finally, a chance arose to question R' Ephraim Zalman about his long walk.

"When I prepare to *daven* each morning," he explained, "I do not wish my thoughts to have the slightest tinge of arrogance. After all, I might boast that I am a scholar, that I am a wealthy man, that not many have attained the things that I have.

"Therefore, before I go to shul, I walk down those two blocks. A great *talmid chacham* lives on the first block, and I am reminded that there is a person who is greater than I in his knowledge of Torah. On the second block lives a very rich man, richer than I. After I see those two, I am certain that I will not come to *davening* with a proud or boastful attitude."

Many tales are told about the tremendous humility of R' Yosef Zundel of Salant. Once, when standing in the marketplace lost in Torah thoughts, he was startled by a sudden cry. "Reb Yid! Reb Yid!"

Turning his head, R' Yosef Zundel saw two merchants standing at the roadside. One of the men wished to sell his horse to the second man.

"How can I help you?" R' Yosef Zundel asked courteously, grateful for the chance to be of service.

"Do you know something about horses?" the first horse dealer asked. "I want to sell this man my horse. Maybe you can give him some pointers?"

R' Yosef Zundel felt no diminution of his honor as he stepped up closer to the horse, examined it in the manner of an expert, and offered his opinion.

Both men were amazed at the depth of his knowledge and understanding. They thanked him with heartfelt gratitude. R' Yosef Zundel parted amicably from them, beaming with pleasure at the mitzvah that had fallen into his lap while he was thinking about something else.

The Gift

וְאִם דַּל הוּא וְאֵין יָדוֹ מַשֶּׂגֶת

"If he is poor and his means are not sufficient"

(Vayikra 14:21*)*

A certain *talmid chacham* was about to move to Eretz Yisrael and came to take his leave of R' Shraga Feivel Frank. On the spot, R' Shraga Feivel took off his expensive fur cape and handed it to his visitor.

At first, the other man refused the gift, but R' Shraga Feivel was at his most persuasive. The cape would be very useful to the man on his long journey to Eretz Yisrael, he said. It would also come in handy once he was living there, especially if he took up residence in Yerushalayim or Tzefas.

"You will need this cape more than I," R' Shraga Feivel insisted. And, in the end, the man was induced to accept it.

Hidden Treasure

כִּי תָבֹאוּ אֶל אֶרֶץ כְּנַעַן אֲשֶׁר אֲנִי נֹתֵן לָכֶם לַאֲחֻזָּה וְנָתַתִּי
נֶגַע צָרַעַת בְּבֵית אֶרֶץ אֲחֻזַּתְכֶם

"When you arrive in the land of Canaan that I give you as a possession, and I will place a tzara'as affliction upon a house in the land of your possession."

(Vayikra 14:34)

"[This is] a good tiding to them, that afflictions are to come upon them, because the Amorites hid treasures of gold in the walls of their houses all forty years that Israel were in the desert, and as a result of the affliction he breaks down the house and finds them." (Rashi)

A young yeshivah man purchased a home that had formerly belonged to an old Jewish woman who had died at the age of 95. He bought the house from the woman's daughter, who was 70, and who was not able to summon the will or the energy to empty the house of its contents before the new owner moved in. She stipulated that the house would be sold together with all its contents (furniture, clothes, etc.), and insisted that this term be written into the contract.

One day, before the young man moved in, his children entered the house. One of them noticed an object protruding from a mattress. Pulling it out, the children saw that it was a metal box, securely padlocked.

When the box was opened, the family was astounded to see that it was stuffed full of cash, bonds, and diamond-studded jewelry. The treasure was worth a great deal of money.

It was clear that the old woman who had previously owned the apartment had not revealed to her family the existence of this treasure. Now, it was very likely that the family had no claim to the box, as the deed of sale had stated clearly that the house was sold along with all its contents.

But the man who had bought the house had no hesitation about which course to take. He would not keep the treasure unless a halachic authority authorized him to do so. He phoned R' Moshe Feinstein and told him the whole story. R' Moshe asked for a little time to look into the matter, and asked the young man to call him again the following day.

When the man phoned again, R' Moshe said, "You are obligated to return everything! The contract says that the house's contents were sold together with the house but this does not apply to cash. People generally sell furniture, clothes, and other objects with a house, but nobody sells a house along with cash! And in this case, the diamonds are also classified as cash, because it is clear that there was no intention to sell them."

The yeshivah man heeded this ruling. He handed over the entire treasure to the previous owner's daughter. Touched and amazed by his honesty, the woman suggested that it was only right that part of the proceeds be distributed to charity for the needy.

The Day the Roof Fell In

וְנָתַץ אֶת הַבַּיִת

"He shall demolish the house"

(Vayikra 14:45)

R' Yaakov Chaim Sofer, author of the *Kaf HaChaim,* was once sitting and learning on the upper floor of a *beis midrash,* when a portion of the building suddenly collapsed. The floor of the room where R' Yaakov Chaim sat was left dangling. In another moment, it would crash down into the *beis midrash* below! Both he and those seated in the room below were in grave danger. Pandemonium erupted.

"We have to save the Rav!" These few people who had not taken leave of their senses crept toward the second floor, to help R' Yaakov Chaim climb down from his dangerous perch.

But the Rav had no intention of scrambling away. "First," he said calmly, "all the children and adults in the room below must be evacuated."

The others hurried to do as he had instructed. Only when all the others had left the crumbling building and reached a place of safety did R' Yaakov Chaim allow himself to be helped down.

The moment his feet touched solid ground, the second floor collapsed and fell, with a thunderous crash, into the empty *beis midrash* below.

פרשת אחרי מות
Parashas Acharei Mos

Picture Perfect

בְּזֹאת יָבֹא אַהֲרֹן אֶל הַקֹּדֶשׁ
"With this shall Aharon come into the Sanctuary"
(Vayikra 16:3)

In addition to delivering *shiurim* and guiding his students in the Torah's ways, R' Aharon Kotler also shouldered the practical burdens of his yeshivah. He would go over the yeshivah's finances regularly, and he personally signed receipts for donations.

One day, a new booklet of receipts was delivered to him. Each receipt bore a picture of the yeshivah building. Attractive trees and flower beds had been added to the picture to enhance the yeshivah's image.

In astonishment, R' Aharon went to see the yeshivah secretary. "I recognize the building and the yard around it but as far as my memory serves these trees and flowers do not exist!"

"That's true," the secretary replied. "They were drawn in by the artist who designed the receipts, to give the place a more attractive appearance and have it make a better impression."

"Lies and deceit are hateful!" exclaimed R' Aharon. "There may be people who will give the yeshivah a larger donation, on the assumption that it costs more to keep up such a campus. This is not right! How can I sign, and consent to, something that is not true?"

Renewed Hope

כִּי בַיּוֹם הַזֶּה יְכַפֵּר עֲלֵיכֶם לְטַהֵר אֶתְכֶם מִכֹּל חַטֹּאתֵיכֶם לִפְנֵי ד' תִּטְהָרוּ

"For on this day he shall provide atonement for you to cleanse you; from all your sins before Hashem shall you be cleansed."

(Vayikra 16:30)

It was Rosh Hashanah, and the entire congregation stood tense and expectant, as they waited for the first shofar blast. But R' Zusha was clearly not ready. Every pair of eyes watched anxiously as, wrapped in his *tallis* in front of the *aron kodesh,* R' Zusha *davened* with bowed head and frequent, heart-rending sighs.

Worried glances were exchanged all through the shul. What was the meaning of R' Zusha's weighed-down stance and the heavy signs?

Suddenly, the Rebbe stirred. He left the shul and went out into the street, to search for a merit that might help the Jews in their time of trouble, a merit that would tilt the scales.

The streets were nearly deserted. Everyone was in shul. The Rebbe peered here and there until he saw, on the corner of the block, a poor small Jewish boy. His clothes were plain, his shoes were torn, and his face was pinched and white with hunger.

R' Zusha approached the boy, stroked his cheek, and asked, "My good child, don't you ever envy the non-Jewish children when you see them lacking for nothing, dressed in beautiful clothes, and eating tasty, healthy food?"

"*Chas v'chalilah!*" the boy shot back at once. "Of course I don't envy them. Just the opposite — I'm happy being who I am, because I am a Jew. It's better to be a hungry Jew than a full *goy*! *Baruch she'lo asani goy* (Blessed [is He] Who did not make me a gentile)!"

Hearing these words, R' Zusha smiled radiantly. He took the child by the hand and led him into the shul. Walking up to the *aron kodesh,* he cried out emotionally, "Our Father in Heaven, Who has chosen His people, Israel, with love — look down and see whether there is another nation like Yours, or if there are children like Your Jewish children in all the world! Here is a small boy whose parents are destitute and cannot provide him with enough food to eat or good clothes to wear. He is dressed shabbily and eats sparingly. Nevertheless, he takes very great pride in his Jewishness, and it would never occur to him to envy gentile children who have enough to eat. On the contrary, he thanks You, Master of the Universe, for making him a Jew, a son of the nation that You have selected from among all the other nations. He blesses You joyously and gratefully: *Baruch she'lo asani goy!*

"Father in Heaven, look down at Your people, Israel, and see how happy they are with You and Your mitzvos!"

Then, with a heart filled with renewed hope, the holy Rebbe raised the shofar to his lips and sounded the first ringing note.

Raised voices emanated from the room where R' Moshe Feinstein was presiding over a *din Torah*.

"I won't pay the money under any circumstances!" one of the litigants shouted.

Everyone present in the room sat rigid with shock. The *gadol hador* (Torah leader of his generation), R' Moshe Feinstein, had ruled that the man must pay. All the power of the Torah lay behind that ruling. How did the fellow dare reject the ruling? Where did he find the nerve to argue so brazenly?

R' Moshe gazed at him benevolently, and asked, "Why do you refuse to pay?"

"Because the ruling is not valid. Money judgments are not supposed to be made at night!"

"What *chutzpah!*" the others thought indignantly. "How dare he make a mockery of R' Moshe's *kavod haTorah* (honor of the Torah)?"

But R' Moshe showed no sign of anger. Calmly and pleasantly, he explained to the litigant that he had made no error in his judgment, that his ruling was correct, and that the man was obligated to pay the money to its proper owner.

Five months later, that same man appeared at R' Moshe's home once again. This time, he had a favor to ask.

"Will the *Rosh Yeshivah* write out a certificate stating that I am an ordained *shochet?*"

R' Moshe picked up his pen and, without the slightest hesitation, began to write. The man, meanwhile, waited in another room.

Those who were with R' Moshe glanced at one another in astonishment. One of them stepped up to R' Moshe and asked, "Does the *Rosh Yeshivah* remember that man?"

"Of course I remember him," replied R' Moshe, without pausing in his writing.

"In that case, the *Rosh Yeshivah* must surely recall the man's terrible behavior."

R' Moshe lifted his head and interrupted forcefully. "What does one thing have to do with the other? Yom Kippur has passed in the meantime, and I said then that I forgive anyone who has sinned against me. My friends, this is no children's game! I said that I forgive him — and I meant it with all my heart!

"Apart from that, the fellow has doubtless repented by now."

And he went out to hand the certificate to his waiting visitor.

One *erev Yom Kippur,* the shul was filled with people ready to begin *Kol Nidrei,* but R' Yisrael Salanter had yet to put in an appearance. They waited a while, but when they saw that the sun was about to set they were forced to recite the *Kol Nidrei* without him.

Afterwards, the congregation waited once more before beginning *Ma'ariv,* but still R' Yisrael did not come. Messengers were sent to search for him at home and on the streets, but no one could find him.

Ma'ariv was nearly over when R' Yisrael suddenly appeared in shul. He wrapped himself in his *tallis* and stood up to *daven.*

Later, he explained his prolonged and mysterious absence.

"On my way to shul, I heard a baby crying inside one of the houses I passed. I went inside and found a baby, just a few months old, lying in his crib and wailing pitifully, a bottle full of milk beside him. Close by sat his sister, a girl of about 6 who had fallen asleep."

R' Yisrael understood that the baby's mother had left her infant in the young girl's care while she went out to shul for *Kol Nidrei,* leaving the bottle of milk prepared for him. The girl, meanwhile, had fallen asleep and did not wake to her baby brother's cries.

R' Yisrael picked up the bottle of milk and fed the baby. Then he settled the baby in his crib to sleep. Only then did he wake the girl, intending to go on to shul. But the girl was frightened at being left alone, and begged him not to go.

R' Yisrael stayed. Only after the mother returned from shul did he take his leave.

In telling the story, R' Yisrael expressed his enormous joy at having had the opportunity, on the holiest night of the year, to perform a *chesed* for two small and helpless children.

A shoemaker once subjected R' Aharon Roth to a scathing verbal attack. He hurled abuse at R' Aharon, who did not say a word in reply. Some time later, on *erev Yom Kippur,* the Rebbe took along several companions and went to see the shoemaker.

Upon their arrival, the Rebbe said, "It's been a long time since I have seen you. I understand that you are undoubtedly angry at me. That is why I have come now, on *erev Yom Kippur* to appease you and ask your forgiveness."

The shoemaker was amazed at the Rebbe's humility. Instead of the shoemaker going to R' Aharon to beg his forgiveness, the Rebbe himself had come to see *him!* The man was filled with shame and remorse — and a boundless love and admiration for the Rebbe.

From that day on, he became one of R' Aharon's most faithful and ardent followers.

The Proper Preparation

שַׁבַּת שַׁבָּתוֹן הִיא לָכֶם וְעִנִּיתֶם אֶת נַפְשֹׁתֵיכֶם

"It is a Sabbath of complete rest for you, and you shall afflict yourselves"

(*Vayikra* 16:31)

It was *erev Yom Kippur,* after *Minchah*. The large *beis midrash* in Mesivta Tiferes Yerushalayim, where R' Moshe Feinstein served as *Rosh Yeshivah,* emptied of people. Everyone hurried home to complete their preparations for the holy day, and to eat the *seudah hamafsekes,* the last meal before the fast.

Then someone noticed the *Rosh Yeshivah,* R' Moshe, working with the elderly *shamash* to empty the shul's *tzedakah* boxes. As they emptied each box they transferred the money to envelopes for distribution to worthy institutions after Yom Kippur.

R' Moshe noticed the man watching him in open surprise. Gesturing quietly at the *shamash,* R' Moshe murmured, "He also has to get home to eat the *seudah hamafsekes* before the fast."

Heaven's Protection

אִישׁ אִישׁ מִבֵּית יִשְׂרָאֵל אֲשֶׁר יִשְׁחַט שׁוֹר אוֹ כֶשֶׂב אוֹ עֵז

"Any man from the House of Israel who will slaughter an ox, or a sheep, or a goat"

(Vayikra 17:3*)*

It was R' Yechezkel Abramsky's custom never to eat meat slaughtered by a *shochet* who had reached an advanced age, even if the *shochet* was still doing a proper job. Wherever R' Abramsky served as Rav, he would have the *shochtim* retire at a certain age.

R' Abramsky once came to serve at a *beis din* in Switzerland. When he reached his lodgings, he asked who the *shochet* was. The innkeeper answered, "There are two *shochtim* here. One is elderly and pious, the other young and newly ordained as a *shochet.*"

R' Abramsky asked to eat meat slaughtered by the younger man.

One day, he was served chicken soup and found an ant swimming in the bowl. He decided not to eat the soup. A little while later, the innkeeper came in with the main course and noticed that R' Abramsky had not touched the soup. R' Abramsky showed him the ant.

That particular hotel was well-known for its cleanliness. When the hotelkeeper saw that, despite all their efforts, an ant had made its way into the soup, he confessed to the Rav that the younger *shochet* had not come to town that day, and he had decided instead to give R' Abramsky the chicken that the older *shochet* had slaughtered. Now, he said with deep feeling, he saw clearly how Heaven had protected R' Abramsky. To keep him from eating meat he did not want to, an ant had fallen into the soup.

R' Abramsky later added a postscript to this story. "When a person undertakes to observe the Torah and be strong in his performance of the mitzvos, Heaven helps him!"

R' Meir Feist would review *Maseches Chullin* every year, as well as the *Shulchan Aruch Yoreh De'ah,* despite the fact that he was already well versed in all portions of the Torah.

When asked why he reviewed these specific portions repeatedly, he would answer, "At a young age I received a *heter hora'ah* (permission to teach), and the certificate says that I am an expert in *Yoreh De'ah.* Because it says that about me, despite the fact that I do not work as a teacher, I must always make sure that these matters — concerning what is permissible and what is forbidden — are clear in my mind!"

※

When R' Meir of Premishlan was 10 years old, he began going to the marketplace in Podheitz every Thursday to collect alms for the poor. He would then distribute the money to those who needed it to buy food for Shabbos.

Once, R' Meir approached a certain butcher and asked for a donation of one thaler.

"Meir'che," said the butcher, "I will give you two thalers, on the condition that you tell me if this ox that I'm thinking of buying is kosher or not."

"If you give me half a *pirtziger* [valued at ten thalers]," the boy replied, "I will tell you what you want to know."

The butcher considered a moment, then agreed. He handed Meir the coin, and Meir said, "The ox is *treif.*"

"Well, what about that one?" the butcher asked, pointing at another one.

"For another half a *pirtziger,* I'll tell you!"

The butcher paid out the money, and Meir said, "That ox is *glatt* kosher."

The butcher was skeptical about whether the boy really knew what he was talking about. But Meir was a pure and pleasant child whom everyone liked, and the butcher knew that the money would go to the poor. He bought the second ox, and another butcher purchased the first. And Meir's pronouncements turned out to be absolutely on the mark: The first ox was found to be *treif* while the second was kosher.

The following week, Meir returned to the cattle market to collect *tzedakah* as usual. His old friend the butcher came over to him at once.

"Meir'che, I'll pay you a full *pirtziger* if you tell me whether all the oxen here are kosher or *treif.*"

"If you give me half a *pirtziger* for each one," the boy calmly replied, "then I'll tell you."

The butcher agreed to Meir's terms. Meir began walking among the oxen, pronouncing one kosher and another *treif* until he had made the rounds of all the cattle. He left the market a very happy boy, because his pockets were full of money to distribute to the needy and he would not have to walk around all day collecting when he would rather be learning Torah.

Seeing that the boy's assessment was always accurate, the butcher approached him yet again on the third Thursday. This time, he had a business proposal. "I want to make a contract with you. Every week I will pay you for each head of cattle, as you wish, but you must agree to keep our deal a secret."

"I have no wish for contracts or secrets," Meir replied. "If you give me half a *pirtziger* for each ox, I'll tell you if it's kosher."

This arrangement continued for the next few months, without anyone being the wiser. Each Thursday the butcher would come over to Meir and pay him in advance. Then the boy would go through all the cattle, telling the butcher which were kosher and which were not. As a result, the butcher grew very wealthy. The other butchers in town were stymied to know how he always managed to pick the kosher cattle.

These other butchers came to complain to the Rav, accusing the local *shochtim* of accepting bribes from the butcher to pronounce all of his cattle kosher and all of theirs *treif*. The elderly *shochet* protested, "But you see, in the slaughterhouse, with your own eyes, that all his animals are kosher! There is no room for the slightest doubt. What can anyone do if he happens to be lucky?"

The butchers were silenced. They had no answer.

In desperation, they began to follow the "lucky" butcher, to see what he did to ensure that all the cattle he purchased were *glatt* kosher. That Thursday, they saw him stroll through the marketplace with a young boy, who was pointing at the various head of cattle. When the butcher left, the others came to Meir and said, "Meir'che, *daven* for us, too, the way you're *davening* for him or do for us whatever you've been doing for him!"

"I don't do anything," Meir replied. "If you give me half a *pirtziger*, I'll tell you."

"But what do you tell him to do? Tell us, and we'll do the same thing."

"He asks me which ox is kosher and which is *treif,* and I tell him."

The butchers handed Meir half a *pirtziger* and gestured at a nearby ox. "That ox is *treif,*" Meir said at once.

They pointed to another ox. "But you only contributed one half a *pirtziger* to *tzedakah,*" Meir reminded them.

The butchers muttered amongst themselves. "Now we know the secret!"

From that day on, all the butchers got together and gave Meir the money he wanted for *tzedakah.* Then they walked with him through the cattle market and he told them which was kosher and which was *treif.*

When Meir's teacher heard about this, he scolded the boy and ordered him not to make any more such pronouncements based on *ruach hakodesh.* The teacher was a chassid of R' Aron Leib of Premishlan, Meir's father. When he next saw R' Aron Leib, the teacher related the entire episode to him, ending with the scolding he had given young Meir.

The *tzaddik* answered, "It was right of you to rebuke him. It is forbidden for the boy to reveal secrets!"

One Mitzvah Leads to Another

וּשְׁמַרְתֶּם אֶת חֻקֹּתַי וְאֶת מִשְׁפָּטַי אֲשֶׁר יַעֲשֶׂה אֹתָם הָאָדָם וָחַי בָּהֶם

"You shall observe My decrees and My judgments, which man shall carry out and live by them"

(Vayikra 18:5*)*

The following story is brought down in the Beis HaLevi's Haggadah. During the period when the Beis HaLevi served as Rav of Slutzk, there came a year when, just days before Pesach, a rich man came to see him secretly. The man confessed that he had suffered grievous business reverses that year, and did not even have enough money to pay for the holiday's expenses. He was too embarrassed by his plight to ask his fellow businessmen for a loan, lest they laugh at him, and he was also afraid that if the fact of his reversals became public knowledge, no one would sell him merchandise on credit and help him get back on his feet. Not knowing where to turn for help in securing a loan, he had come to the Rav himself.

The Beis HaLevi was filled with compassion for the man. He gathered together every last penny he could find, both his own money and the money that others had left with him, and gave it to the businessman. The Beis HaLevi's joy was, if anything, even greater than the borrower's.

The Beis HaLevi made one condition: The man must not reveal to a soul that he had received the loan. Because the Beis HaLevi had given away the last cent he had available to him, anyone else who came seeking a loan would have to be turned away empty-handed. Also, since it would be better for the businessman if his reputation as a wealthy man remained intact, secrecy was the best policy.

But the businessman, greatly moved by the Beis HaLevi's compassionate act, could not refrain from telling others in the community about the generous loan he had received. The news took wing, and many others began to flock to the Rav's house seeking similar loans or handouts. The Rav's coffers were empty, forcing him to take out other loans himself in order to meet the demand. Troubled, he commented that the businessman had not behaved according to the condition of the loan — or with wisdom.

Hearing this, the Beis HaLevi's 7-year-old son who would later become world famous as the Brisker Rav asked, "Father, why are you so distressed? Didn't we learn in *Maseches Avos* that one mitzvah drags along another one? The spread of this story will lead to many mitzvos of *tzedakah* and *chesed*."

The Rav smiled at the youngster's wisdom, and took his innocent words to heart.

A Just Reward

וּשְׁמַרְתֶּם אֶת חֻקֹּתַי וְאֶת מִשְׁפָּטַי אֲשֶׁר יַעֲשֶׂה אֹתָם הָאָדָם וָחַי בָּהֶם אֲנִי ד'

"You shall observe My decrees and My judgments, which man shall carry out and live by them — I am Hashem."

(Vayikra 18:5)

"I am Hashem, Who is faithful to pay reward." (Rashi)

R' Yitzchak Eizik of Safrin was especially devoted to the important mitzvah of *pidyon shevuyim*, redeeming Jewish prisoners. On one occasion, an opportunity came to him to perform this mitzvah and he did so with all his resources to the point of giving away all his property.

One Shabbos, a coach came to a halt near R' Yitzchak Eizik's house in a Polish village. Inside were two Jewish girls who had been taken prisoner by a local *poritz*. The girls' father had leased a tavern from the *poritz,* but had fallen far behind in his payments. The debt totalled hundreds of gold coins, an enormous amount in those days. The *poritz* seized the man's two daughters as security for his payment.

R' Yitzchak Eizik's pity was profoundly stirred by the girls' plight. He decided to redeem them at any price.

Because it was Shabbos, R' Yitzchak Eizik went to the non-Jewish village elder, bringing along his only cow as security. In tears, he begged the elder to help him by assuring the *poritz* that he, R' Yitzchak Eizik, would personally repay the tavern-keeper's debt right after Shabbos. Being familiar with R' Yitzchak Eizik's integrity, the elder agreed to act on his behalf and deal with the *poritz*. The girls were freed.

As soon as Shabbos was over, R' Yitzchak Eizik sold all the merchandise in his store, all the grain in his barn, and his only cow, until he had the sum required to pay the debt. He handed the money to the *poritz* in exchange for the girls' liberty.

R' Yitzchak Eizik and his wife, Hinda, found out, however, that the girls' father had died of anguish, and took the two sisters into their home. They raised the girls as their own.

After paying so lavishly to liberate the girls, R' Yitzchak Eizik and his wife had nothing left. One day a visitor came to their home, but there was not so much as a piece of bread with which to honor the guest. R' Yitzchak Eizik and his wife were greatly grieved at their inability to perform the mitzvah of *hachnasas orchim* as in former days. Hinda went to her neighbor, borrowed a bit of food from her, and prepared a meal for the guest.

Just before the visitor left, he spread his hands and blessed the couple, who were childless, to merit having sons who would grow up to be *geonim* and *tzaddikim* who would light up the world with their Torah.

The blessing was fulfilled. R' Yitzchak Eizik and his wife raised five sons to be Torah greats: R' Tzvi Hirsch of Ziditchov, author of the *Ateres Tzvi,* R' Moshe of Sambor, author of the *Tefillah L'Moshe,* R' Alexander Sender of Komarna, R' Yissachar Berish of Ziditchov, and R' Lipa of Sambor.

Six Gold Coins

וּשְׁמַרְתֶּם אֶת מִשְׁמַרְתִּי

"You shall safeguard My charge"

(Vayikra 18:30)

Every Purim, one of the city of Brody's wealthy residents would send R' Shlomo Kluger a gold coin along with his *shaloch manos*. One year, the man changed his custom and sent six gold coins instead. R' Shlomo sent five of them back, keeping only one for himself.

When his family expressed surprise at this, R' Shlomo explained.

"It is clear to me, almost beyond the shadow of a doubt, that this man has some matter to bring up with me, and it was his intention to bribe me with this extra money so that I would take his side when he needs me. He knows that if he would come offering a bribe, I would refuse to take it. Instead, he thought he would trick me into taking one by sending it ahead of time with the *shaloch manos*!"

Not a week later, R' Shlomo's family was able to witness his wisdom firsthand. The same rich man who had sent the *shaloch manos* with the extra gold coins came to the house with a request: He wanted R' Shlomo to give a Pesach *hechsher* (certificate of *kashrus*) for a certain drink that he had imported from a distant place.

"*Baruch Hashem*, Who enlightened my eyes and made me be suspicious of the rich man from the start!" R' Shlomo thought happily.

As for the *hechsher,* R' Shlomo did not provide one, as the drink was not kosher for Pesach!

פרשת קדושים
Parashas Kedoshim

A Mother's Command

אִישׁ אִמּוֹ וְאָבִיו תִּירָאוּ
"Every man shall revere his mother and his father"
(Vayikra 19:3)

The two holy brothers, R' Shmelke of Nikolsburg and R' Pinchas author of the *Hafla'ah,* once decided to travel to the city of Chortkov to gladden their mother's heart with a visit, and to demonstrate to her the reverence she deserved. Their mother was filled with joy when she received a letter containing the date of their planned visit.

The news that the two great Rebbes were about to descend on them spread through Chortkov as if on wings. Excitement gripped the city. From every corner, people streamed out, on foot and by wagon, to greet the brothers.

When the mother heard about the abundant honor that was about to be heaped upon her and her two sons, she rushed to send them a message: "My sons, by the respect you have for me as your mother, I command you: Go home and do not come visit me!"

This order caused no little surprise. The mother explained, "I do not want to take pleasure from my honored sons in this world. I prefer to receive my full reward in the World to Come!"

The brothers, receiving the message, obeyed their mother's command without question. Though it was difficult for them to give up the visit, they returned home because that was what their mother wanted.

They had planned to go see her in order to demonstrate their respect for her — but because she had ordered them *not* to come, refraining from the visit now became the proper way to show their reverence.

Even as a child, R' David of Lelov loved every Jew with a fierce and overflowing love. When his father bought him a warm winter coat one year — a coat that he really needed — young David was overjoyed. And yet, the very next day, when he met a poor boy who was shivering from the cold, he was overcome with pity. Immediately, he took off his coat and put it on the boy's shoulders.

When David returned home without his new coat, his mother asked if he'd forgotten it in *cheder*. He had no choice but to tell her the truth.

"Go back to that boy at once and take back your coat," she said, "before your father finds out about it and punishes you."

But David answered calmly, "I am prepared to be punished. I can even fulfill the mitzvah of *kibbud av* by preparing a stick that Father can use to hit me, to save him the trouble of finding one. But I cannot hurt that poor boy and take back the coat I gave him!"

On another occasion, as a young boy, R' David traveled to Lizhensk for the first time to see the Rebbe Elimelech. His father was upset that David had undertaken the trip alone, without his parents' knowledge, and wanted to beat him as a punishment.

The boy looked about the house with his eyes, then ran outside. He searched the ground until he found a stick, and ran back indoors with it. He handed the stick to his father, saying, "Do not trouble yourself with searching, Father. Here is a stick to hit me with."

A Fortified Wall

לֹא תִּגְנֹבוּ
"You shall not steal"
(Vayikra 19:11*)*

The Sfas Emes used to tell the following story about his childhood.

"When I was a boy, my grandfather, the 'Chiddushei HaRim,' took me to the Kotzker Rebbe's house. One day, I heard my aunt complaining to the Rebbe's assistant, R' Feivel, about some things that had been missing from the house. Apparently, they had been stolen.

"'Is that any wonder?' R' Feivel answered. 'And why shouldn't they steal? Everything in this place is *hefker*!'

"The Kotzker Rebbe heard what R' Feivel had said. He raised his own voice. 'Why shouldn't they steal? Everything is *hefker*? But the Torah explicitly states: *Lo signovu! — You shall not steal!*'"

The Sfas Emes added, "That shout pierced my heart. The words, '*Lo signovu*' must stand like a fortified wall, so that no man dare reach out a hand to steal."

As a young boy, the Chofetz Chaim was once playing with his friends when a peddler woman came by, a basket of apples over her arm. Suddenly, the basket overturned and the apples tumbled out.

The youngsters, including young Yisrael Meir, seized the opportunity to grab a few apples as they rolled away on the ground. With good appetite they fell on the fruit, paying no heed to the outrage they were perpetrating on the unfortunate woman.

A few days passed. Yisrael Meir was sitting and learning *Chumash* with his father when they reached the verse, "*Lo signovu* — You shall not steal.*" All at once, the incident with the peddler woman and her apples came rushing back to Yisrael Meir's memory. The boy could find no peace. He had transgressed an explicit prohibition in the Torah! What to do?

Yisrael Meir asked his mother for a penny. He went over to the peddler woman and bought a number of apples from her. He paid the price of the apples — and then returned them to the basket and ran away.

Years later, when R' Elchonon Wasserman — the Chofetz Chaim's foremost student — heard this story, he said, "We can see from this tale that from the moment the Chofetz Chaim began to become aware, as a young child, he learned the Torah for the sake of observing it. That was his greatness!"

R' Nosson Adler was once looking out of his window when he saw a thief load a bundle of sticks onto his shoulder — sticks that he had just stolen from the woodpile in R' Nosson's own backyard. R' Nosson ran outside and chased the thief, crying out, "You are fortunate, Reb Yid! You are lucky that Heaven gave me the privilege of seeing what you did. This way, I was able to declare the wood *hefker* (ownerless), and you are not transgressing the prohibition of *Lo signovu!*"

Startled and confused, the thief threw down the bundle of sticks. R' Nosson said promptly, "Now, Reb Yid, you have given me the opportunity to merit another mitzvah, *Azov ta'azov imo.*"

With that, he went over to the bundle of sticks, lifted it up, and replaced it on the thief's shoulder!

Fair Wages

לֹא תַעֲשֹׁק אֶת רֵעֲךָ
"You shall not cheat your fellow"
(Vayikra 19:13*)*

R' Zusha of Anipoli was extremely destitute. He devoted all his energies to Torah and Divine service, and had no source of livelihood. His wife was accustomed to making do with very little, wearing the same old clothes year after year.

At long last, however, she felt she needed a new dress, and asked her husband for the money to buy fabric. With great effort, R' Zusha managed to secure a loan for the required amount. His wife went happily to the tailor's shop, bringing along the newly purchased material. But just a few days later, she looked sad once more.

R' Zusha asked why she wasn't happy.

"The tailor is very poor," she explained. "His daughter has been engaged for some time, but he still has no wedding clothes or other dowry for her. As he sewed my dress, I saw that he looked very miserable. When I asked him what was wrong, he told me that the *chasan* had seen the dress and thought it was meant for his *kallah*. When he heard that it was intended for one of the tailor's customers, he became very angry.

"I stood up and told the tailor that the dress was his daughter's — a complete gift. And now, I am left without a new dress."

R' Zusha heard his wife out, then asked, "Tell me, did you pay the tailor for his work?"

"No," answered his wife gloomily. "After all, I gave him the entire dress!"

Trembling, R' Zusha asked, "How could you cheat a man of his just wages? That poor man was waiting eagerly for his wages, in order to buy food for his hungry children. Is he to blame if you decided to leave the dress in his hands? He needs money!"

The Rebbetzin, hearing this, agreed with her husband. She ran over to a neighbor, borrowed the necessary sum, and went to pay the tailor his wages at once.

R' Eliyahu Dushnitzer, *mashgiach* of the Lomze Yeshivah, was always extremely careful about money matters. The yeshivah provided him with electricity for his meager home. In his later years, when he sat up learning late into the night, he would light a kerosene lamp and turn off the electric light, saying, "In my old age I have to be concerned lest I doze off over my *sefer* and the light remains burning unnecessarily at the yeshivah's expense."

Once, R' Eliyahu brought his Shabbos coat to a tailor for mending. That Friday he went back to the tailor to get the coat, and paid the man for his work.

On his return home, he noticed that the tailor had sewn an extra button onto his coat without being instructed to do so. Because R' Eliyahu had not paid him for that button, he was afraid he might be transgressing the prohibition against stealing. There was no time to go back to the tailor before sundown, so that Shabbos, he did not wear the coat.

On another occasion, he attended a *Kiddush* at a man's home. As he prepared to leave afterwards, he asked to speak to the woman of the house. He blessed her warmly, then added, "When I made *Kiddush* on the wine, a few drops may have spilled onto the tablecloth. In that case, please forgive me. And if others did the same thing, do me a favor and forgive everyone!"

The woman answered, "They are forgiven" — and R' Eliyahu's eyes sparkled with joy.

Extra Pay

לֹא תָלִין פְּעֻלַת שָׂכִיר אִתְּךָ עַד בֹּקֶר

"Payment for the work of a hired worker shall not stay overnight with you until morning."

(Vayikra 19:13)

R' Yehoshua Leib Diskin's wife once hired a porter to carry a heavy package to her home. She paid him for the job and he went on his way.

When her husband came home, he saw the package and asked his wife how much she had paid the porter to carry it. She told him.

"The price should have been higher," R' Yehoshua Leib declared.

Immediately, his wife took the amount of money needed to make up the difference, and sent it to the porter by messenger. The hour was late and the streets were dark. It took the messenger considerable effort to find the porter's residence. But find him he did, at last, and paid him the additional money that R' Yehoshua Leib had decided was due him.

The time for lighting the Shabbos candles was fast approaching one Friday, when the Chofetz Chaim was seen wandering through one of Warsaw's side streets. Witnesses were amazed and bewildered by this strange behavior. It turned out that one of the printers who had worked on the Chofetz Chaim's *sefer* that *erev Shabbos* had been absent when wages were paid. In order not to transgress the mitzvah of "You shall pay his wages on that day" and the prohibition against leaving a worker's wages overnight, the Chofetz Chaim had asked the man's fellow laborers where the printer lived, then hurried to his house before candlelighting to pay him what he owed.

The Chofetz Chaim's daughter remembered a time when her father woke her in the middle of the night to ask her to accompany him to a certain tailor's house in order to pay him his wages, which the Chofetz Chaim had forgotten to pay that evening. The tailor's home stood at the edge of town, and the night was frigid. But the

Chofetz Chaim said, "It's nothing, it's all worthwhile, the main thing is not to transgress what the Torah prohibits."

One winter day, the Chofetz Chaim traveled by coach from Radin to the train station. On the way, he suddenly remembered that he had forgotten to pay the tailor who had mended his coat. At once, he asked the driver to take him back to Radin, so that he might pay the tailor that same day.

When asked later why he hadn't simply sent the money back with the driver, who lived in Radin, instead of going all the way back himself, the Chofetz Chaim replied, "When the matter touches on a prohibition from the Torah, one does not rely on a messenger."

After *Minchah* one day, R' Eliyahu Dushnitzer, *mashgiach* of the Lomze Yeshivah in Petach Tikvah, gave an electrician a lamp for some minor repair. The electrician generally *davened* in the yeshivah. When he came to *Ma'ariv* that same night, he brought the repaired lamp back with him, along with the resolve not to ask for payment for such a minor job.

R' Eliyahu took a long time over his *tefillah,* so the electrician decided to go over to the *mashgiach's* apartment, near the yeshivah, and leave the lamp there.

The next day, when the electrician came to the yeshivah before dawn to learn, he was surprised to find R' Eliyahu waiting for him, money in hand. Disturbed, the *mashgiach* demanded, "Is paying a worker on time a light thing in your eyes — or is the prohibition of *lo salin* against leaving a worker's wages overnight a matter of no consequence?"

The Case of the Missing Coin

בְּצֶדֶק תִּשְׁפֹּט עֲמִיתֶךָ
"With righteousness shall you judge your fellow."
(Vayikra 19:15)

The Kesav Sofer, Chief Rabbi of Pressburg, worked hard to persuade the Hungarian government to recognize the Orthodox community as a separate entity. His goal was to keep it well away from the insidious influence of the Reform movement. He sought a separate framework for the Torah-observant community, based only on the *Shulchan Aruch*.

When he succeeded at last, everyone knew that his triumph was the fruit of seeds planted by his father, the Chasam Sofer, who had struggled mightily to organize and unite religious Jews under the banner of Torah. The Kesav Sofer invited all of Hungary's Torah leaders to a festive celebration, with the aim of strengthening and guarding the spiritual life within their communities.

Attending the celebration were the cream of Hungarian rabbinical Jewry. The place was filled with Torah debates and the atmosphere was elevated. At last, the Kesav Sofer rose to the podium. Into the respectful hush, he began to speak.

"My teachers and *rabbanim*! On this significant occasion, I would like to show all the honored guests something important that was given to me by my father, *zt"l*. He himself inherited this thing from *his* father, and so on back through the generations, to the time when the *Beis Hamikdash* stood.

"Though this thing has no inherent value in itself, we still cherish it as a precious object — an object of inestimable value. I am speaking of a *shekel hakodesh* that was used during the time of the *Beis Hamikdash*. As far as I know, this is the only coin of its kind to be found in the Jewish world today.

"On this festive occasion, I would like to show this coin to the revered guests, who are doubtless interested in seeing it. I will pass it amongst you so that everyone can have a look."

Indeed, interest in the coin ran very high. Every guest there inspected it carefully and respectfully. For a considerable time, the coin passed from hand to hand. Suddenly a voice rang out. "Where is the *shekel*?"

The coin had disappeared!

The Kesav Sofer stood up in great agitation. How had such a thing happened? He turned to the assembled audience and said, "I am certain that the *shekel* has been lost without evil intent on the part of anyone in this room. Therefore, I would like to ask everyone to forgive me, and to check through the coins in your pockets to see if the *shekel* has fallen in among them."

The guests did as he asked, but the *shekel* did not come to light.

Seeing that his first plan hadn't worked, the Ksav Sofer asked for unanimous agreement to a second plan: Every man was to search his neighbor's pockets. But one elderly guest protested vehemently against this suggestion. This man was an exceptional Torah scholar and a former *talmid* of the Chasam Sofer. He pleaded with the Kesav Sofer to wait a quarter of an hour before implementing his plan.

The crowd was forced to accede to the old man's wishes. When 15 minutes had passed with no sign of the missing coin, the man stood up and asked for another quarter of an hour.

The assembled guests, very impatient by this time, objected to this strange request. It seemed utterly illogical to them. But the Kesav Sofer, who knew the old man as one of his own father's venerable students, asked the crowd to yield to his wishes.

When the second period of time had passed with no results, the others began to direct their suspicions toward the elderly *talmid chacham* himself. But the old man begged, with tears in his eyes, that they wait yet another quarter of an hour. He promised that he would not ask them to wait again.

Without the Kesav Sofer's personal intervention, the others would not have agreed. As it was, they grudgingly accepted another wait. This one was even more fraught with tension than the previous ones had been. Soon, however, the door opened and the Kesav Sofer's *shamash* entered the room, holding something aloft.

"Here's the coin!" he cried.

The *shamash* explained to the assembled guests that earlier, when shaking out the tablecloth, he had apparently shaken the coin out together with the garbage. Now, passing the spot again, he had found the coin lying among the leftover food he had tossed away.

Everyone's attention went quickly back to the elderly *talmid chacham*. They were burning with curiosity to hear the answer to the riddle of his strange behavior. Respectfully, they asked him to explain.

The man stood up. "I am a *talmid* of the Chasam Sofer. When I received the invitation to participate in this important assembly, a gathering of Hungary's great men of Torah, I thought that it would be a good idea to bring along something that would interest everyone. I, too, own a *shekel* dating from the time of the *Beis Hamikdash*. It, too, has been in my family for generations. I decided to take the coin along to show it to all of you here today. But when I heard my Rebbe's son, the Kesav Sofer, speak about the value of the coin in his keeping, I decided out of respect for him to keep silent about my own coin.

"Then the coin was missing, and the notion was raised of having each man search his neighbor's pockets. It was clear to me that the 'missing coin' would be found in my pocket! You can imagine the tremendous *chillul Hashem* that would have resulted from such a thing. Imagine if the lost coin would have been found in the pocket of one of the Chasam Sofer's students!

"I was certain that telling you all that I also owned such a coin would have been useless. I would not have been believed. Therefore, I tried with all my might to push off the search, while at the same time praying with all my heart to *Hakadosh Baruch Hu* not to heap such a humiliation on my head or to cause me to be the instrument of such a grave *chillul Hashem*.

"My prayers were answered, and the coin was found. Here is the holy *shekel* that I own!" And he lifted up his coin.

When the man had finished speaking, the Kesav Sofer turned to the assembly and said, "We must thank *Hashem Yisbarach* for bringing this matter to a successful conclusion and preventing a *chillul Hashem*. Indeed, who would have believed him? Everyone was convinced that there was not another coin like this in the world!

"In addition, this episode must teach us how far to take the Torah's injunction to judge every person favorably. Even in a situation that seems, according to all the information available to us, to point to a certain person's guilt — even then, we must make every effort to judge him innocent.

"If we have only come together today to learn this one valuable lesson — *dayenu* (it is enough)!"

Murder ...

לֹא תֵלֵךְ רָכִיל בְּעַמֶּיךָ
"You shall not go about gossiping among your people"
(Vayikra 19:16)

    R' Aharon of Karlin set off on foot to see his Rebbe in Mezritch. On the road, he was picked up by a group of wagon drivers who offered him a ride. As they rode along they traded gossip and slander about all the Jews in town. R' Aharon interrupted their stream of talk by asking a question about horses, and the group enjoyed an animated discussion of horses all the way to Mezritch.
    As the wagon rolled into town, it was engulfed on every side with chassidim. The drivers were astounded. Turning to R' Aharon, they asked, "If you are a Rebbe, why did you talk about horses with us all the way here?"
    "I saw that your talk was murdering people," R' Aharon answered dryly. "Better that you should kill horses."

The Right Moment

וְלֹא תִשָּׂא עָלָיו חֵטְא
"You shall not bear a sin because of him."
(Vayikra 19:17)
"Do not make his face pale [by reproving him] in public." (Rashi)

    "It is preferable for a person to hurl himself into a burning furnace rather than embarrass his fellow in public" (Berachos 43).
    It was preferable for R' Shlomo Zalman Auerbach to place himself in a position of danger rather than embarrass someone, even someone who had done something he should not have done, and richly deserved to be rebuked.
    R' Shlomo Zalman was once traveling in a young man's car. A

second passenger, a student in the yeshivah, was also riding with them. To their distress, the young driver began to speed and to drive recklessly. Suddenly, the car crashed into a retaining wall. Miraculously, none of the passengers were hurt. R' Shlomo Zalman sat trembling, but he uttered not a word. Not a single word!

When they finally arrived at their destination, R' Shlomo Zalman waited until the student who had traveled with them had left the car. Only then did he address the reckless driver, reprimanding him for risking the lives of three people and asking him to promise to drive more carefully from then on.

"You should know," R' Shlomo Zalman added severely, "that from the first minute you began driving unsafely, I wanted to get out of the car and walk. But I didn't want to humiliate you in the other boys' eyes."

Loving Strangers Like Family

וְאָהַבְתָּ לְרֵעֲךָ כָּמוֹךָ
"You shall love your fellow as yourself"
(Vayikra 19:18*)*

R' Menachem Mendel, the Vizhnitzer Rebbe, had a daughter who once became gravely ill. She lived far from her parents' home at the time. Every day, a telegram was sent to her father, containing the latest news on her medical condition.

One day, no telegram arrived. The Rebbe paced the rooms of his house, his entire being consumed with pain.

"Father, don't worry! The mail is probably late. Do not fear the worst," pleaded his son, R' Baruch.

Indeed, before long the daily telegram was delivered. Then, during the afternoon, an additional telegram arrived with the welcome news that the danger had passed. With Hashem's help, his daughter would recover completely. A smile of vast relief spread over R' Menachem Mendel's face.

Gathering his courage, his son asked, "Father, is it possible that a person like you can become upset or anxious if a telegram is late?"

The Rebbe gazed upon his son and answered, "I have always

worked on improving my *middos* to elevate them to a holy level. In general, this has not been too difficult for me — except in the area of *v'ahavta l're'acha kamocha* ("You shall love your fellow as yourself"). There, I have been unable to reach the level I have been aiming for.

"I thought that I had finally reached the level where I am able to care for every Jew the way I care for myself and my loved ones. But today, I discovered the truth. When the telegram did not come and I heard no news, I became very agitated and I learned how far I am from attaining the level of *v'ahavta l're'acha kamocha*. I receive letters by the dozens every day, each of them containing requests and information about other Jews' illnesses and difficulties. Do I worry about those the way I worry about my only daughter?

"I suddenly realized how far I am from attaining the level of '*kamocha* — as yourself.' *That's* why I was so upset!"

R' David of Lelov's son once fell gravely ill. The townspeople, fearing for the boy's life, gathered in shul to *daven* on his behalf. They also visited the patient and labored devotedly to care for him in his illness. After some time, the boy recovered and began to grow strong again.

The townspeople expected, naturally, to find R' David bursting with joy. Instead, they were stunned to see him crying.

"When my son got sick," R' David explained, "everyone wished him well, *davened* for him, and worked to take care of him until he recovered. But had it been just any Jew who'd fallen ill, no one would turn the world over. No one would have cared. That is certainly something to cry about."

While studying in Rebbe Shmelke's yeshivah, R' Moshe Leib of Sassov decided that he wished to attain the heights of prayer reached by R' Levi Yitzchak of Berditchev. R' Levi Yitzchak was like a burning flame when he *davened*. R' Moshe Leib went to Rebbe Shmelke and asked him to help him reach his goal. The Rebbe answered that R' Levi Yitzchak had been guided by his teacher, the great Rebbe of Mezritch. He was the proper person to guide R' Moshe Leib now.

R' Moshe Leib traveled to Mezritch. The Maggid of Mezritch was an aged man by this time, and no one was permitted to see him, except those seeking an answer to the most difficult halachic questions for which the city's *dayanim* had found no solution.

R' Moshe Leib entered into a complex halachic discussion with the *dayanim,* debating with them at length until they decided to bring the question to the Maggid for resolution. Thus, R' Moshe Leib gained entry to the Maggid.

The Maggid raised his eyes and looked at R' Moshe Leib. "What do you want?," he asked.

R' Moshe Leib answered at once, "I would like the Rebbe to teach me how to attain the level of *tefillah* of R' Levi Yitzchak."

"In my old age," answered the Rebbe, "I do not have the strength to do this. But I will not send you away empty-handed. Listen, and I will tell you a story from which you will be able to learn the path to *avodas Hashem* (Divine service)." And the Rebbe went on to tell the following tale.

There were once two faithful friends. One became prosperous while the other became destitute, but their love and loyalty to each other remained steadfast. The poor man did not envy the rich one. Their unconditional love grew only stronger.

Then, one day, a robbery took place in the king's treasure house — and suspicion fell on the poor man. He was thrown into prison and sentenced to death.

The news came to the rich friend's ears. He went to the king's court and tried to exert his influence to save his friend. After a great deal of effort, the king finally told him, "If you wish to offer your life in place of his, I will set your friend free."

Without hesitation, the rich man agreed to these awful terms. He took upon his own head the decree that had been set against his friend, and was prepared to die in his friend's place. When his poor friend heard this, he objected violently, and refused to change places under any circumstances. The matter reached the point where the two faithful friends were arguing with each other about who would sacrifice his life for the other!

When the king saw this, he told the friends, "I will lift the death sentence and free the prisoner — but I ask you to let me join in your friendship."

The Maggid finished his parable. "This story symbolizes the Torah's command, 'And you shall love your fellow as yourself, I am

Hashem.' When Hashem sees great love among his Jewish children, He wishes to join them and be counted as their friend."

R' Moshe Leib came away from Mezritch with his path marked clearly before him: to devote himself wholeheartedly to cultivating *ahavas Yisrael,* an abiding love for his fellow Jew. He became outstanding in this mitzvah; not only did he preach *ahavas Yisrael,* he practiced it beautifully as well, caring devotedly for each and every member of the Jewish people.

R' Aharon Rokach, the Belzer Rebbe, had just emerged from the bathhouse.

"Please bring me a cup of coffee," he asked his assistant. "But a *good* cup of coffee — with cookies!"

The aide was bewildered. He could not believe what his ears had just heard. A "good" cup of coffee? The Rebbe was always extremely minimal in his eating. He tasted nothing all day. Only after midnight did the assistant bring him a bit of challah and soup and even then it had happened more than once that he had found the challah and soup the next morning, exactly where he had left them.

A "good cup of coffee"? Where had the request come from — and why in the world did the Rebbe want cookies?

The aide hurried to fulfill the Rebbe's request. On his return, however, his astonishment grew even greater. The Rebbe asked him to bring the coffee and cookies over to Reb Berel, the tailor.

The assistant was at a loss. He knew of the Rebbe's tremendous love for his fellow Jew. Once, when a thief had broken into the Rebbe's house on a Friday and was caught and arrested, the Rebbe had ordered *Kiddush* wine, two loaves of challah, and a lavish Shabbos meal to be sent to the thief's prison cell. "He is a Jew," he had explained.

But why was the Rebbe suddenly interested in serving coffee and cookies to a simple tailor? The assistant was determined to unravel the mystery.

With the coffee and cookies set out on a tray, he walked over to Reb Berel's house. He knocked gently on the door and then entered, carefully placing his offering on the table.

"This is for you," he told the astonished tailor. "The Rebbe sent it."

"Coffee and cookies from the Rebbe — for me?" Reb Berel exclaimed in amazement. "But — why?"

The coffee's good aroma reached his nostrils. Suddenly, a broad smiled appeared on the tailor's face. He had remembered.

"About half an hour ago, I was in the *mikveh*. The Rebbe was also there. When I stepped out, refreshed, I blurted, "Ah, how good it would be, after immersing in the *mikveh*, to drink a good cup of coffee with some tasty cookies. It would be a lifesaver!"

Reb Berel's smile grew even wider. As for the Rebbe's aide, he was enormously moved. The Rebbe had never tasted a "good cup of coffee" and yet he knew how to provide a "lifesaver" for others. How incredibly great was his love for his fellow man!

"It Hurts!"

וּבֶגֶד כִּלְאַיִם שַׁעַטְנֵז לֹא יַעֲלֶה עָלֶיךָ

"And a garment that is a mixture of combined fibers shall not come upon you."
(*Vayikra* 19:19)

A student of R' Aryeh Leib HaKohen, author of the *Ketzos HaChoshen*, told this story.

"When my Rebbe became ill and weak near the end of his life, I once had the honor of tending to his needs. He lay without strength, to the point that I had to put on his socks for him. I didn't ask any questions; I merely went over, picked up a pair of socks that were lying nearby, and put them on his feet.

"When I had finished, I was stunned to hear the Rebbe, who barely had the strength to speak, suddenly let out a shout like a roar. 'It hurts! It hurts!'

"Flustered, I thought in my innocence that something in the socks was actually piercing the Rebbe's feet. I went over, took the socks off his feet, turned them inside out, and put them on again. But this time, too, he roared out, 'It hurts! It hurts!'

"Suddenly, I realized that he was referring not to physical pain, but to a spiritual one. The socks were probably *shaatnez*.

"And so it turned out. I sent them to be checked at once, and saw with my own eyes that the woolen socks were sewn with flaxen threads!

"Our Rebbe had a pure and holy body. In his holiness, he was

Kedoshim / 131

able to sense a spiritual 'piercing' which allowed him, even in his weakened state, to let out a roar like a lion!"

When R' Ze'ev Chechik was admitted into a Jerusalem hospital, he would talk to no one nor find any rest, until an expert had been summoned to check all the hospital sheets and gowns for *shaatnez*.

He entered the hospital a very sick man — a man who feared he was on the brink of death. But on his admittance he forgot all that, and was interested in one thing only: *shaatnez*.

The book *Pillar of Fire* tells the story of the events leading up to R' Yehoshua Leib (the *Maharil*) Diskin's arrest.

An irreligious Jew went to the police with an accusation against the Maharil Diskin. Very shortly afterward, the police showed up at the *tzaddik's* home. The Maharil lifted himself slowly from his chair, put on his coat, and recited the blessing, "*Baruch Dayan emes*" ("Blessed is the true Judge"). The entire street stood watching in awe.

As he prepared to climb into the police coach, R' Yehoshua Leib noticed that its interior was upholstered in *shaatnez*. He refused to enter.

The officers were forced to bring a different coach. Seeing that this one contained no *shaatnez*, the Maharil climbed aboard and sat down, the radiance of the *Shechinah* shining from his face.

It is said that the Steipler, R' Yaakov Yisrael Kanievsky, took a very long train trip as a youth. The train's seats were upholstered. From fear that the upholstery might contain *shaatnez*, the Steipler refused to sit down, but stood on his feet for the entire journey.

On another occasion, when the Steipler was living in Moscow, he was drafted into the Czar's army. He was based in an area where the weather regularly plunged down to 30 degrees below zero. But because he was afraid that the army's military coats might contain *shaatnez*, the Steipler refused to wear one. The others were at a loss to understand his behavior. At last, however, they took him to a military warehouse and let him choose a summer uniform to wear instead.

It was the Steipler's habit, from his youth, to distance himself from even the whiff of a halachic question or doubt. One day, when he was learning in the Navoradok Yeshivah, he heard some of the other students discussing a suspicion of *shaatnez* that had been raised about the lining of their coats.

Immediately, the Steipler arose from his seat. Without a word, he went over to his coat, ripped out the lining, and sat down again to resume his learning.

When the Mirrer Yeshivah relocated to Shanghai, China, during World War Two, its students and faculty were constantly guarded by Heaven from stumbling in the area of *shaatnez*.

Once, on Yom Kippur, one of the students left in the middle of *davening* and returned a short time later, dressed in weekday clothes. Being caught up in the holiness of the day, no one asked him the reason for his behavior. That night, however, he was questioned by his curious friends.

"I felt that my *davening* was not going well. I tried to arouse myself, I read *mussar* books, but nothing helped. Then I remembered reading, in an introduction to a certain *sefer,* that *shaatnez* prevents prayers from being accepted by Hashem. As it says in the *sefer* "*Tzioni,*" in reference to *Parashas Kedoshim*:

"'*Shaatnez* symbolizes the two prosecuting powers above who speak against the nation of Israel, whom *Hashem Yisbarach* separates. When a person wears *shaatnez,* he combines those two powers and confuses Israel's prayers. [Our Sages] have said that when a person wears *shaatnez* while *davening,* his prayers are not accepted along with the rest, as he appears as an idol worshiper that is lending power to the forces of impurity.'

"I suspected that the new shirt I was wearing may contain *shaatnez*. That was why I went to my room and changed into the old clothes I had brought with me from Lithuania. Then a light shone in my soul, my *davening* began to go smoothly again, and my devotion and enthusiasm were appropriate for the holy day!"

The shirt was given to an expert, who found that it did, indeed, contain *shaatnez*. (It is important to note that the student had given it to be checked by a mitzvah-observant tailor before Yom Kippur, but the tailor was ignorant of the modern-day complications of *shaatnez*. There are numerous places where flaxen threads may be found, and there is also some flax that is woven in a special way that makes it hard to identify.)

This episode raised doubts in the Mirrer students' minds about other clothes. From then on, every new article of clothing was submitted to an expert for a thorough examination for *shaatnez*.

Man Is Like a Tree

וּנְטַעְתֶּם כָּל עֵץ מַאֲכָל
"And you shall plant any food tree"
(Vayikra 19:23)

It was the night of Tu B'Shevat, and a large gathering of chassidim surrounded the table of R' Yosef Meir of Spink. At the head of the table sat the Rebbe, explaining the significance of the New Year for trees. He spoke of the things that men and trees have in common.

"With great effort and the investment of much energy, one can help a tree grow — even a crooked one that has lacked nourishment and water. Sometimes, through devoted and persistent care, we can turn a stunted tree into a blooming one."

At that moment, a bearded and well-dressed Jew entered the room. He walked over to the table and set down a gigantic basket bulging with choice fruits. Looking up, the Rebbe spotted the guest and broke into a broad smile. He invited the man to sit beside him and showed him the most remarkable warmth all through the evening. None of the chassidim knew the stranger's identity. Who was this man who had brought such a stunning fruit basket and had been honored by such tokens of the Rebbe's affection?

Afterwards, the chassidim heard the story from the guest himself.

"I was born in Germany," he said, "and arrived here only a few years ago. The education and upbringing I received at home were completely divorced from any connection to Torah and mitzvos. My father and grandfather identified with the *Haskalah* (Enlightenment) movement in Germany, and raised me accordingly.

"On my arrival here, I opened a textile factory. At first I sold my goods only in the surrounding area, but success soon smiled on me and my business expanded greatly. I sent my merchandise to every part of the country and even to neighboring countries. Everything was wonderful.

"Then tragedy struck one morning. I purchased an enormous quantity of raw material at an exceptionally low price, and was already mentally counting up the tremendous profits I expected to make from the deal. I paid for all the materials in cash and returned to my office. I was sitting there, dwelling pleasurably on the successful deal I had just concluded, when the supplier of the materials suddenly walked into my office and demanded payment for what he had sold me.

"At first I thought he was joking. Very soon, however, it became clear that I had fallen into a trap. I remembered that the man had not signed a receipt for the money I had paid him. What remained was the contract, signed by me, authorizing the materials to be transferred and obligating me to pay for them.

"Furious, I threw the man out of my office, but he was unmoved by my anger. Before he left he informed me that he planned to sue me in court. I sat slumped in my seat, feeling frustrated and helpless. It was clear to me that he would win the case in court, and instead of the vast profits I had anticipated, I would soon be a poor man. In very low spirits, I went outside for a breath of fresh air.

"In the street, I ran into an acquaintance and told him all about the misfortune that had just occurred to me. He suggested that I accompany him to see his Rebbe and ask for advice. In my despair, I was ready to agree to anything.

"I'll never forget the glow in the Rebbe's eyes on the evening I was first privileged to enter his room. I could not conquer the tears that insisted on coursing down my cheeks, and managed only with difficulty to tell the Rebbe what had befallen me. When I finished my story, the Rebbe turned to me and asked if I was Sabbath observant. I barely knew what Shabbos was, and did not attach much significance to his question. I explained that a good deal of my business was done on

Shabbos, making it impossible for me to refrain from working on that day.

"The Rebbe went on to ask if I was careful to eat only kosher food. I answered in the negative, justifying myself by saying that my many business pressures prevented me from paying attention to such details.

Then the Rebbe asked if I at least put on *tefillin*. Once again, my answer was no.

"The Rebbe began to try to persuade me to put on *tefillin* every day. 'If you agree to put on *tefillin* each morning,' he said, 'I guarantee that you will emerge from your court having won your case.'"

"After much inner debate, I agreed to the Rebbe's request and left him with a lighter heart. And from that day on, I began to faithfully put on *tefillin* every day. It wasn't easy for a man like me, and sometimes I nearly stopped — until I remembered the Rebbe's promise. One mitzvah pulls another along in its wake, and the mitzvah of *tefillin* dragged me along to begin observing other mitzvos.

"My day in court arrived. It was Tu B'Shevat, exactly one year ago today. My chances of winning the case seemed nil, but I went to court in comfortable spirits, inexplicably placing my trust in the Rebbe's promise.

"The supplier portrayed me as a cheater, a man who had taken his material and then refused to pay. To back up his claim, he presented the contract I had signed. I then took the stand and told the truth, that I had paid but had not received a receipt. I don't know how to explain it, but the judge was persuaded of the truth of my story, and acquitted me of any wrongdoing.

"From that day on, my offices are closed on Shabbos. Not only has this not harmed my interests, but business has boomed! I have begun to live a full life of Torah and mitzvos, though I am not an actual chassid."

The man smiled joyously at his rapt audience. "Today, on the anniversary of the day when I won my court case because of the Rebbe — and when I was, so to speak, reborn — I thought it proper to bring the Rebbe a basket of the best fruits."

A Source of Blessings

וְהָדַרְתָּ פְּנֵי זָקֵן
"And you shall honor the presence of an elder"
(Vayikra 19:32)

There was a poor old widow who lived in the Steipler's neighborhood. One day, the woman broke her leg and was in need of daily care until the leg mended. One of her neighbors took the widow into her home for that period. The neighbor's husband, who was close to the Steipler, told him the story.

The Steipler was very moved by the man's wife's generosity in taking in the widow. "From now on, we can send people to her for a *berachah*, as her blessings will undoubtedly come true since she is involved in this tremendous mitzvah of hosting and caring for a widow!"

The widow used to have a girl sleeping over so she would not be alone at night. The girl became engaged to an excellent *talmid chacham*. The girl's father came to tell the Steipler the news.

"Do you know why your daughter merited a *chasan* who is a *talmid chacham*? Because of the great mitzvah she is fulfilling by staying with that widow!"

❦

At the conclusion of the First World War, R' Baruch Dov Leibovitz, author of the *Birkas Shmuel*, traveled with his family by train from Kremenchug to Poland. Army troops were everywhere. At one of the stations, an old woman and her daughter wanted to board the train but the soldiers did not allow them on, forcing the two women to remain behind at the station.

Seeing them standing on the platform, R' Baruch Dov decided not to travel further. "I will not leave an old woman and her daughter among killers!"

At once, he and his entire family left the train and remained on the platform until another train arrived. Then R' Baruch Dov, his family, and the old woman and her daughter boarded the new train together.

פרשת אמור
Parashas Emor

Honesty — the Best Policy

וְלֹא תְחַלְּלוּ אֶת שֵׁם קָדְשִׁי וְנִקְדַּשְׁתִּי בְּתוֹךְ בְּנֵי יִשְׂרָאֵל

"You shall not defile My holy Name, and I shall be sanctified among the Children of Israel"

(Vayikra 22:32)

The Chofetz Chaim was accustomed to *davening Shacharis* at dawn, during both winter and summer. One morning, for a legitimate reason, he was late getting to shul. As he walked in, he found several of his students ready to leave the shul, their own *davening* already completed.

Stopping them on their way out, the Chofetz Chaim began to apologize. "I was late for *Shacharis* today only out of necessity."

His students were taken aback. "Does the Rebbe think he owes us an apology? Does he think that we suspect him of unworthiness? If the Rebbe came late to *davening,* it's clear to us that something urgent came up!"

"My dear students," the Chofetz Chaim replied. "I knew that you did not suspect me, but I wished to teach you to be very careful never to do anything that might bear an unworthy appearance in another's eyes. Such an act can bring about a diminishing of the Torah's honor and a *chillul Hashem.* It is better to apologize and to explain your actions over and over, rather than to ever be the cause of a *chillul Shem Shamayim* (a desecration of Heaven's Name)."

R' David Luria (the Radal) of Bichov was falsely accused of rebellion against the king.

After several days in jail in Petersburg, the Radal was interrogated by high government officials. During the interrogation, the

officials began speaking amongst themselves in French, certain that their prisoner understood nothing of the language. But the Radal's integrity forbade him from eavesdropping on a confidential discussion under false pretenses. Wordlessly, he stood up and went to stand in a distant corner of the room.

"Why aren't you sitting in your place?" one of the officials shouted angrily.

Smiling, the Radal turned to the man and said, in French, "I saw that you were speaking to each other in French in order to keep what you were saying a secret from me — but I know the language. My conscience did not allow me to listen to things that you do not wish me to know. I do not wish to be a thief."

The Radal's honesty stunned the officials. From that moment, he found favor in their eyes, and was eventually acquitted of all the charges against him. The Radal was rewarded for the wonderful *kiddush Hashem* that he had made.

The Chofetz Chaim was once hurrying to catch a train to Vilna for a very important purpose. On his way down the street, someone came out of a house of mourning and asked him to be part of a *minyan* for *Minchah*.

Despite the fact that his trip to Vilna was so important — *and* the fact that the Chofetz Chaim himself had already *davened Minchah* — he decided to do as the man asked.

Of course, he missed his train and was forced to wait for the next one. However, it was all worthwhile, in the Chofetz Chaim's view — to prevent a *chillul Hashem*!

R' Zalman Sorotzkin once traveled by train to Navoradok, together with another Rav. The two were traveling on a mission to rescue certain Jewish souls. They were well on their way when a snowstorm struck. Mounds of snow quickly covered the roads, and the train progressed only with great difficulty. Finally, it was forced to a complete halt.

The second Rav glanced at his watch and told R' Sorotzkin worriedly, "It's a short Friday today, and Shabbos comes early."

"The train can't go on because of the heavy snow on the tracks," someone explained. All the passengers descended to help clear the tracks of snow. Then they climbed back aboard, and the train continued on its way — but not for long. The heavy storm continued, dumping vast quantities of snow on the train and the tracks. At about noon, the train finally reached a way station. The conductor called for a special crew to clear the tracks, and the train was on its way once again.

They all hoped to make quicker progress now, but were doomed to disappointment as the heavy snowfall quickly re-filled the tracks. The train moved sluggishly at best, and was forced to stop frequently for the tracks to be cleared again and again. The hours sped by. Shabbos was approaching fast, and Navoradok was still a considerable distance away.

"Even the next station is some distance from here," the second rav said to R' Sorotzkin, "but we have no choice but to stay in the train until we reach it. It would be endangering our lives to get out in a snowstorm in the middle of nowhere and try to get to the next town on foot."

R' Zalman Sorotzkin gazed out the window. The falling snow obscured his view, but he managed to spot some houses in the distance. There was a place of habitation not too far away! It was time to leave the train now, before Shabbos descended and spread its wings. But this place was between stations. Would the conductor agree to let them off?

He hurried over to the conductor. "Would you like a bottle of whiskey?"

The man's eyes lit up.

"In that case," R' Zalman continued, "stop the train so that we can get off!"

R' Zalman took a coin out of his pocket and dangled it in front of the conductor, who immediately brought the train to a screeching halt.

A freezing wind blasted into their faces as R' Zalman and his companion stepped down onto the snow-filled road. Headed directly into the wind, they began to wade through the drifts. The swirling snow obscured their vision. Darkness was falling. The Rabbis progressed at a snail's pace toward the village lights twinkling in the distance.

"We'll knock on the first door we see," said R' Sorotzkin. "What can we do? We'll have to spend Shabbos in the home of a non-Jew.

On *motza'ei Shabbos* we'll continue on our way. The main thing is to get a roof over our heads and walls to protect us from the cold and the snow."

At long last, a house loomed up before them, shafts of light streaming from its windows. The Rabbis approached the house and looked into the window.

Imagine their astonishment when they saw that the light that had beckoned to them from afar was the light of Shabbos candles on a beautifully set table.

That Shabbos, R' Zalman and his friend sat not at a gentile's table, but in the home of a Torah-observant Jewish farmer!

Just One Prayer

וְנִקְדַּשְׁתִּי בְּתוֹךְ בְּנֵי יִשְׂרָאֵל

"And I shall be sanctified among the Children of Israel"
(Vayikra 22:32)

The *sefer "Zichron Yaakov"* relates an incident that occurred in the year 5600 (1840). During that time, Jewish children were snatched by soldiers of the Russian Czar and forced to serve in the Russian army for tens of years, far from their families and their own people. These Jewish conscripts suffered bitter ordeals if they wished to guard their heritage.

St. Petersburg did not yet have a regular shul at that time, but only a chapel where Jewish soldiers in the Russian army prayed. That year, R' Yitzchak Blazer, the *Tzemach Tzedek* of Lubavitch, and other notable rabbinic figures gathered in St. Petersburg to try to influence the Czar on behalf of their Jewish brethren. It was Yom Kippur, and they *davened* together with the Russian soldiers.

When they reached *Ne'ilah*, the illustrious guests suggested that one of their number lead the congregation in this prayer.

The military men objected.

"Of course that would be nice. But we have one soldier here who has sanctified *Shem Shamayim* (Heaven's Name) as much as the greatest leaders of Israel, and has withstood great challenges and ordeals in a truly awesome way.

"Look at his skin," the soldiers continued, "and you will see that it is filled with scars and craters from the numerous beatings and tortures he has suffered at the hands of those who wanted him to abandon his religion! Heroically, he has withstood tortures that would have broken complete *tzaddikim*.

"Therefore, in our opinion, there is no worthier man to lead us in the *Ne'ilah* prayer than this man, who has created such a public *kiddush Hashem!*"

At the urging of all those present, the man consented to let them take a look at his skin. When the Rabbis saw it, they trembled. "Let him stand up for us! We have no *shaliach tzibbur* more worthy than he. May his prayers be accepted on High!"

The man stood up before the ark, but before he began to recite the *Kaddish* before the *Amidah*, he called out in a shaking voice, "Master of the Universe! What do people generally *daven* for? They pray for three necessary things: for children, for life, and for support. But we — all of us here — have a different agenda.

"Regarding children — as soldiers, we are not married. As for life — our deaths would be sweeter than such a bitter existence! And as for our support, we have a Czar who takes care of that for us.

"We have one thing to pray for — just one thing:

"*Yisgadel v'yiskadesh shmei rabba* — May Your blessed Name be raised up high."

Business Can Wait

וּבַיּוֹם הַשְּׁבִיעִי שַׁבַּת שַׁבָּתוֹן מִקְרָא קֹדֶשׁ כָּל מְלָאכָה לֹא תַעֲשׂוּ
"And the seventh day is a day of complete rest, a calling of holiness, you shall not do any work"
(*Vayikra* 23:3)

R' Salman Mutzafi enjoyed telling the story of a *kiddush Hashem* that occurred on the holy Shabbos day.

That Shabbos, one of Iraq's highest treasury officials arrived with urgent haste at R' Mutzafi's office. The official was accompanied by the British Consul, as well as a delegation of top-level businessmen who had come from England to conclude an important business deal. In light of the vital nature of the matter, the gatekeeper was sent over to R' Mutzafi's home to fetch him.

Not finding him there, the gatekeeper went to the *beis midrash,* where he discovered R' Mutzafi sitting and learning R' Chaim Vital's *"Etz Chaim"* together with his teacher, R' Yehudah Pesaya. Totally immersed in the most elevated of matters, R' Mutzafi was wrenched away by a summons to engage in secular matters with gentiles on Shabbos!

Hearing the summons, he thought at first, "What do I have to do with them?"

Then, suddenly, he had a second thought. "I will go and make a *kiddush Hashem!*"

R' Mutzafi's Shabbos garb was different from that of the rest of the week. On Shabbos, he wore a silk robe with a white coat over it, and a light-colored turban on his head. Dressed this way, he rose and went to his office.

When he walked in, everyone stood and bowed respectfully. He took his watch from a cabinet. The watch was set to Israeli time, and its hands stood at 10 o'clock. R' Mutzafi turned to the assembled group and said, "The sun will set in two hours, and about three-quarters of an hour after that the Shabbos Queen will depart and I will be able to attend to you gentlemen. I am a Jew, and I observe my G–d's commandments!"

His simple and candid declaration took the others by surprise. The British Consul said, "We respect your religion and your honesty. We will wait here until your Sabbath is over!"

The Rav returned to his teacher, almost dancing with joy. He had never felt the holiness of Shabbos as much as he did that day, knowing that ten or so dignitaries awaited him, each of them now aware that there is a *Shabbos kodesh* in the world, that it was given as a sign by the Creator Himself, and that the Jewish nation observes the Shabbos and is pledged to maintain its existence forever!

The Shabbos Shopkeeper

שַׁבָּת הוּא לַד' בְּכֹל מוֹשְׁבֹתֵיכֶם
"It is a Shabbos for Hashem in all your settled places."
(Vayikra 23:3)

R' Soloveitchik once spoke of the Bais Yaakov that had been established in his city of Brisk, in the heart of a nonreligious neighborhood. One of the families in that neighborhood preferred to send their daughter to the Bais Yaakov for the convenience of its proximity to their home, despite the fact that the family was not mitzvah-observant. The parents, in fact, publicly desecrated the Shabbos. They owned a housewares shop which was regularly open on the holy Shabbos day.

The parents once went out of town on a Friday, planning to stay over Shabbos. Their daughter who attended the Bais Yaakov was left behind, with instructions to open the store and attend to it on Shabbos while they were away.

The daughter was in a quandary, unsure what to do. Finally, she decided that she could not simply refuse to do her parents' bidding. She would open the store and sit there, but she would make every effort not to sell anything on Shabbos.

The parents left, and the daughter put her plan into motion. She opened the store and sat quietly. After a while, a non-Jew entered the shop and asked the price of a small bowl he had seen in the window. The bowl was worth a mere one-and-a-half zlotys.

The girl looked up and said, "That bowl costs 100 zlotys!"

Furious, the gentile stormed out of the store.

An hour later, he returned to say that he was prepared to pay five zlotys, or even ten, but no more. But the girl stood firm: not less than 100 zlotys!

The gentile went away again — only to return every few hours, all through that Shabbos, to raise the price he was willing to pay. But the girl kept refusing to sell the bowl for less than the stated price: 100 zlotys.

Finally, the gentile returned on *motza'ei Shabbos* and agreed to pay the 100 zlotys. He explained, "I know that it is illogical to pay 100 zlotys for a thing that's worth perhaps a zloty and a half. It's just

that I've recently redecorated my home, and when I passed by your store today and saw that bowl, I decided that it matched my new furniture perfectly. I just had to have it! That's why I've finally decided to pay the ridiculous price you're asking."

The following day, on her parents' return, the girl told them the whole story and handed them the 100 zlotys she had received on *motza'ei Shabbos*. And eventually, in the merit of their daughter's respect for Shabbos, the parents, too, became *shomrei Shabbos*!

The Belzer Rebbe Takes a Stroll

וְעִנִּיתֶם אֶת נַפְשֹׁתֵיכֶם בְּתִשְׁעָה לַחֹדֶשׁ בָּעֶרֶב מֵעֶרֶב עַד עֶרֶב תִּשְׁבְּתוּ שַׁבַּתְּכֶם

"And you shall afflict yourselves; on the ninth of the month in the evening — from evening to evening — shall you rest on your rest day."
(*Vayikra* 23:32)

The chassidic Belzer dynasty has been a powerful one for generations. R' Yissachar Dov Rokach, the third Belzer Rebbe, had tens of thousands of chassidim who clustered faithfully around him. Many of them came to *daven* with him on the High Holy Days.

One Yom Kippur afternoon, the atmosphere in the large shul was charged with holiness. Rosh Hashanah had passed, as well as the Ten Days of Repentance, all of them filled with the Rebbe's penetrating and fiery talks. Day by day, the chassidim had felt their hearts open more, and sensed themselves rising on the rungs to true *teshuvah*.

That afternoon, the chassidim, though weak with fasting, were flying high in the special and holy atmosphere. The Rebbe's face glowed with a holy light and his eyes burned as though his soul were floating on higher planes.

Then the Rebbe began his customary "stroll" among his chassidim. Each year, he walked among the worshipers' benches, his hands concealed in the pockets of his coat and his eyes raking each man in turn.

The chassidim's teeth began to chatter with fear. "Our Rebbe can see very clearly," the Belzer chassidim often said. "He sees which of us has done full *teshuvah* on Yom Kippur, and which has not."

The Rebbe passed from bench to bench, hands in his coat pockets and his gaze alighting on every person in turn. When his eyes rested on a man, that man would feel his very soul quake with fear. Who wanted the Rebbe to discover that he had not yet fully repented?

Suddenly, in the midst of his "stroll," one of the more elderly chassidim began to feel the ill effects of his fast. His face grew pale, his legs refused to bear his weight, and his head began to spin, until he nearly fainted. The Rebbe went over to him at once, took his hands out of his pockets, and placed a morsel of cake into the chassid's mouth. The elderly chassid revived at once.

Only then did the secret of the Rebbe's yearly Yom Kippur stroll reveal itself. In the late afternoon of that holy day, though he spent all of it wrapped up in Divine service, he did not forget the welfare of his chassidim. He cared not only for their souls, but also for their frail bodies. He stood ever ready to help them — and to support their souls and their bodies together.

The Test

חַג הַסֻּכּוֹת שִׁבְעַת יָמִים לַד'
"The Festival of Sukkos, a seven-day period for Hashem"
(*Vayikra* 23:34)

One year, just after Sukkos, two boys came to the Chasam Sofer's yeshivah at Pressburg to be tested for acceptance to the yeshivah. Both boys took the test, after which the Chasam Sofer informed them that only one of them had been accepted.

The decision surprised the yeshivah's *Rebbeim,* who had been present at the testing. They asked the Chasam Sofer why he was willing to accept only one of the boys into the yeshivah.

"I sat by my window and watched the two boys as they made their way from the street to the yeshivah," the *Rosh Yeshivah* replied. "On the sidewalk was a pile of *s'chach* that had been removed from a *sukkah.* The first boy paid the *s'chach* no attention, and stepped right on it as he walked. The second boy, however, was mindful of the *s'chach* and walked around the pile.

"Seeing this, I arrived at the conclusion that a boy who is capable of stepping on *s'chach* immediately after the close of Sukkos is not sufficiently sensitive to the holiness inherent in the mitzvos. I don't want a boy like that in my yeshivah. Let him find a different place to learn!"

Anticipation

וּלְקַחְתֶּם לָכֶם בַּיוֹם הָרִאשׁוֹן פְּרִי עֵץ הָדָר כַּפֹּת תְּמָרִים וַעֲנַף עֵץ עָבֹת וְעַרְבֵי נָחַל

"You shall take for yourselves on the first day the fruit of a tree of splendor, fronds of date palms, and branches of a cordlike tree, and brook willows"

(Vayikra 23:40)

R' Levi Yitzchak of Berditchev had the custom of remaining awake all through the first night of Sukkos, eagerly awaiting the moment when he could perform the mitzvah of *netilas lulav*.

At daybreak, he would run, pick up his *lulav* and *esrog*, and recite the blessings over them with tremendous happiness and devotion.

Once, on the first day of the festival, R' Levi Yitzchak hurried to pick up his *esrog*, which was lying in its box inside a glass cabinet. As he reached out, the glass broke and cut his hand. But he felt nothing, no pain at all, as he performed the mitzvah in the grip of a powerful joy.

R' Moshe of Lelov sailed to Eretz Yisrael at a time when such journeys by boat were lengthy and extremely arduous. The trip would take months, one of which would be the month of Tishrei. R' Moshe took along a shofar with him, as well as the *arba'ah minim* and lumber with which to erect a sukkah on board ship.

As the days went by, R' Moshe took great pains to care for the *arba'ah minim*, and keep them fresh. A few days before Sukkos, however, he saw that, although the *lulav, esrog,* and *hadasim* were fine, the *aravos* had decayed to the point that they could no longer be used for the mitzvah. R' Moshe went to the captain of the ship, and asked whether he could stop at a port where it would be possible to obtain another set of *aravos.*

The captain laughed at him. "Do you honestly expect me to change our whole route just so you can buy a few branches?"

"I'll pay you well for your trouble," R' Moshe said. He mentioned a very large sum of money as compensation.

The captain changed his tune. He sailed to a nearby island where *aravos* were to be found. With great joy, R' Moshe was able to fulfill the mitzvah of *arba'ah minim,* even on board a ship!

Waiting for Mashiach

וּלְקַחְתֶּם לָכֶם בַּיּוֹם הָרִאשׁוֹן פְּרִי עֵץ הָדָר

"You shall take for yourselves on the first day the fruit of a tree of splendor"

(Vayikra 23:40)

R' Zalman Baharan was one of the great *geonim* of Yerushalayim. Once, a Jew came to show R' Zalman his *esrog* which, though large and beautiful, was *cha'seir* — that is, it was missing a small chunk. R' Zalman said that, for this reason, the *esrog* could not be used on Sukkos.

The man was astonished.

"What if it is *cha'seir*? This year, an *esrog* like this one is kosher!" (That year, the first day of Sukkos would fall out on Shabbos, when one does not recite the blessing over the *arba'ah minim.* On the remaining days of the festival, an *esrog* of this type, with a small piece missing, is permitted for use.)

Shocked, R' Zalman replied, "Don't you believe in the coming of the *Mashiach*? We await him every day, and when he comes we will all ascend to the *Beis Hamikdash* in great joy. In the *Beis Hamikdash* we make the blessing over the *lulav* and *esrog* even on Shabbos. Thus, on the first day of the holiday, an *esrog* that is *cha'seir* is *pasul* — disqualified for use in the mitzvah."

The Much-Blessed Esrog

פְּרִי עֵץ הָדָר
"The fruit of a tree of splendor"
(Vayikra 23:40)

One year, the Chasam Sofer acquired an especially fine *esrog*. No one had ever seen such a beautiful specimen, and the news of this marvelous *esrog* spread quickly through the city. Great numbers of people came to the Chasam Sofer's home to recite the blessing over his *esrog*.

During *Shacharis* the following day, the Chasam Sofer lifted the *esrog* from its box and discovered that it was no longer beautiful at all. Its sheen had dulled and blackened from contact with the many hands that had held it the day before.

Those *davening* near him watched the Chasam Sofer carefully. What will the Rav say? How will he react to the sight of his once-beautiful *esrog*? He will undoubtedly be very upset.

To their surprise, as the Chasam Sofer looked at the *esrog*, turning it slowly from side to side, his eyes lit up.

"An *esrog* over which so many Jews have recited the blessing — an *esrog* that has been held in so many loving hands — *that* is a splendid and beautiful *esrog*!"

A Beloved Mitzvah

בַּסֻּכֹּת תֵּשְׁבוּ שִׁבְעַת יָמִים
"You shall dwell in booths for a seven-day period"
(Vayikra 23:42)

A heavy downpour was falling outside when R' Mordechai of Lechowitz heard a knock at his door. Opening it, he saw a man drenched from head to toe standing on his doorstep, his threadbare clothes testifying to the fact that he was destitute.

"What can I do for you?" R' Mordechai asked gently.

"I heard," said the poor man, "that your honor collects boards each year for distribution to the needy. It is now *erev Sukkos,* and I have nothing with which to build my *sukkah!*"

R' Mordechai was distressed at having to inform the poor man that all the boards he had collected had already been given away. Sadly, the poor man walked off to continue his search for lumber in the heavy rain, through the muddy streets.

Seeing this, R' Mordechai burst into tears.

"*Ribbono Shel Olam!* See how beloved the mitzvah of *sukkah* is to the Children of Israel! See how dedicated they are to performing it! Rain is falling heavily outside right now, and the city streets are a muddy mess, but that poor man is searching for boards in order to fulfill the mitzvah of building a *sukkah!* Look down from Your holy place in Heaven and spread the *sukkah* of Your peace over Your people!"

When he had finished his prayer, R' Mordechai climbed onto the roof of his house, found a number of stray boards, and quickly sent his servant after the poor man, with instructions to help him build a *sukkah.*

פרשת בהר

Parashas Behar

The Mitzvah Garden

וְשָׁבְתָה הָאָרֶץ שַׁבָּת לַד׳
"The land shall observe a Shabbos rest for Hashem."
(Vayikra 25:2)

The Belzer Rebbe, R' Aharon Rokach, fulfilled the mitzvah of *Shemittah* in unusual ways when the land of Israel rested during the seventh year.

The Rebbe was a very holy man, and his entire being was dedicated to Hashem's service. He was like the ladder in Yaakov Avinu's dream whose feet rested on the ground, while its head rose into the sky.

One day, his followers were astounded to hear that R' Aharon wished to hire a gardener to prepare a beautiful garden beside his house. The chassidim speculated about the Rebbe's motives in wanting such a garden, but no one claimed to really understand what they were. That very day, a gardener was hired to begin work.

When the Rebbe was informed that the gardener had completed the job, R' Aharon issued orders for the man to continue caring for and maintaining the garden in the accepted fashion. A year passed. The month of Elul arrived, along with its aura of fear and repentance that enveloped everyone who came to the Rebbe's house. On the eve of Rosh Hashanah, as great throngs of people stood by the door to the Rebbe's room, waiting for his blessing, R' Aharon called his helper and asked him to inform the gardener that this was to be his final day of work. The Rebbe did not want him to continue caring for the garden any longer.

Now, at last, the mystery of the garden was revealed. On the first day of Tishrei, the year of *Shemittah* would begin. The Rebbe had hired a man to work in his garden for a full year before, so that when the *Shemittah* year came, he could fulfill the mitzvah of "the land shall observe a Shabbos rest for Hashem," by no longer caring for the garden.

Human Error?

שְׁנַת שַׁבָּתוֹן יִהְיֶה לָאָרֶץ
"It shall be a year of rest for the land."
(*Vayikra* 25:5)

The booklet *Kedushas Shevi'is* relates a story that highlights the special Heavenly protection that accompanies those who take care to properly observe the laws of *Shemittah*:

An Egyptian cargo vessel stopped as it neared the shores of Eretz Yisrael. It was the year 5719 (1959). The Egyptian sea captain had made a navigational error. When the crew realized that they were approaching Israeli territory, they quickly let down the lifeboats and slipped away under cover of night. The boat, and its cargo, fell into Israeli hands.

That year was a *Shemittah* year. Every week, the *Shemittah* committee did its very best to provide *Shemittah* observers with the vegetables they needed to sustain themselves. But despite all their efforts, they had not succeeded in obtaining one thing in adequate quantities: onions. There were just not enough onions for the many people who needed them.

The Egyptian ship was loaded with vast quantities of onions. When the ship fell into Israeli hands, so did the onions. The *Shemittah* committee — after considerable effort — managed to have all those onions allocated to the *Shemittah* observers.

"A person does not bruise his finger down below unless it was decreed from Above." The sea captain's error actually led him in the *correct* direction — the direction that Heaven had decreed he was to take.

The Unseen Hand

וְהָיְתָה שַׁבַּת הָאָרֶץ לָכֶם לְאָכְלָה
"The resting of the land shall be yours to eat"
(Vayikra 25:6)

It was the year 5718 (1958), the year before the *Shemittah* year. That summer was comparable to a Friday afternoon. On Moshav Komemiyus, workers labored feverishly to plant, sow, and store animal fodder while they still could. By the time *Shemittah* 5719 (1959) spread its holy wings over the land of Israel, the moshav would be ready for the Shabbos year.

The hay, planted for use as animal fodder, flourished that summer. In just a few days it would be cut down and stored to provide food for the animals during the *Shemittah* year. One morning, several residents of the moshav knocked urgently on the door of their Rav, R' Binyamin Mendelson, and informed him that locusts were coming. The locusts posed a grave danger to the entire crop that had been planted and tended with such dedication.

They were all familiar with their Rav's simple and powerful faith in Hashem. Calmly, he comforted his flock: "Stand up and witness Hashem's salvation this very day!"

Hordes of locusts swarmed into the area, forming heavy dark clouds that covered the sky to the south, and soon descended on the fields. But when the waves of locusts reached Moshav Komemiyus, they halted — as though an unseen hand had stopped them in their tracks. In a short time, the clouds turned to face in the opposite direction. Not a single locust landed in Komemiyus.

Hashem's salvation can come like the blink of an eye!

"Eretz Yisrael Will Be Spared"

וִישַׁבְתֶּם עַל הָאָרֶץ לָבֶטַח
"And you shall dwell securely on the land."
(Vayikra 25:18)

During World War Two, when word came that the German enemy was poised to invade Eretz Yisrael, R' Shlomo of Zvil cried oceans of tears as he prayed fervently to the Creator to spare His people. Each night, he woke to recite the *tikkun chatzos,* head bent to his knees and weeping without pause for hours on end.

To his concerned friends, he would say confidently, "Eretz Yisrael will be spared."

As the Nazis advanced closer and closer to Eretz Yisrael, R' Shlomo's *tefillos* grew more and more intense. R' Shlomo walked around very pale, seized by an indescribable fervor. And yet, at the same time, he continued to hold firm in his opinion that the Nazis would not reach the shores of Eretz Yisrael.

On the 26th day of Iyar, in the year 5705 (1945), the world heard the news: In an unexpected reversal, the Germans had been defeated and were retreating from the gates of Palestine. Throughout the land, shopkeepers closed their stores and spent the day rejoicing in their sudden liberation from the Nazi threat. And on that very same day, R' Shlomo of Zvil departed this world.

The man who had struggled so mightily on behalf of each individual and the community as a whole, the man who had dedicated his life's blood to battling the Nazi enemy, finished his war on the day the enemy fell. His job was done. His soul rose to Heaven on the forty-first day of the counting of the *Omer,* which corresponds to *yesod she'b'yesod.* And while great throngs of people rejoiced in victory, broken-hearted Jerusalemites accompanied R' Shlomo of Zvil to his resting place.

A Meal for the Rebbe

וַאֲכַלְתֶּם לָשֹׂבַע
"And you will eat to satisfaction"
(Vayikra 25:19)

On the day that R' Chaim was to begin serving as *Av Beis Din* of Sanz, he arrived in that city before dawn. After *davening Shacharis*, the city's Torah scholars came in an endless stream to talk Torah with R' Chaim, coming and going all through the day.

Near evening, the chassid, R' Yosef Rafeh, one of the Rebbe's oldest friends, noticed that no one had remembered to give R' Chaim anything to eat. As a result, the Rebbe had not tasted a morsel all day. R' Yosef hurried home and returned a short time later with a dish of potatoes which he concealed beneath his clothes.

"I must speak with the Rebbe on an urgent matter," he said. R' Chaim stopped the Torah discussion he was immersed in, and went into a private room with R' Yosef.

R' Yosef closed the door behind them, and asked the Rebbe to eat the food he had prepared for him. R' Chaim ate, and thanked R' Yosef for his thoughtfulness. R' Chaim was on the verge of collapsing, but in his tremendous absorption in Torah, he had not noticed, until R' Yosef had interrupted his learning.

Enough for Three Years

וְכִי תֹאמְרוּ מַה נֹּאכַל בַּשָּׁנָה הַשְּׁבִיעִת הֵן לֹא נִזְרָע וְלֹא נֶאֱסֹף אֶת תְּבוּאָתֵנוּ
"If you will say: What will we eat in the seventh year? — behold! we will not sow and we will not gather our crop!"
(Vayikra 25:20)

In the year 5712 (1952), the Jewish Agency decided to plant orchards in several settlements throughout Israel. One of the designated orchards was slated for Moshav Komemiyus.

The moshav's residents stipulated one condition: No work was to be done in the orchard during the *Shemittah* year. The Jewish Agency rejected this condition, and the planting of the orchard was delayed. Though efforts were made over time to come to an agreement, the issue of *Shemittah* stood like a rock in the negotiators' path. No agreement was reached.

In 5718 (1958), the year before a *Shemittah* year, the moshav's Rav had a lengthy discussion with the Jewish Agency administrator in charge of the orchard plantings. Eloquently, the Rav explained the significance and the holiness of *Shemittah,* how beloved it is to Hashem, and how inextricably it is linked to the coming of the *Mashiach.* The Jewish Agency man, caught up in the Rav's enthusiasm, authorized the planting of an orchard in Komemiyus in which all the laws of *Shemittah* would be faithfully observed, in accordance with the Rav's instructions.

The orchard cost the Jewish Agency about half a million *lirot.* The *Shemittah* came in the second year after its planting, when young saplings require constant care. This care was tendered only at the Rav's orders. Those responsible at the Jewish Agency warned the Rav that he was endangering the orchard and that the entire investment was likely to be lost, but the Rav was firm in his faith in Hashem, in the merit of the mitzvah of *Shemittah.*

In the month of Av, near the end of the *Shemittah* year, the Jewish Agency administrator in charge of the orchards came to see the Rav, highly excited. He said that, out of the twelve orchards in his care, only one of them — the one planted in Moshav Komemiyus — observed the laws of *Shemittah.* And it was this very orchard that had flourished more than all the others!

"How can you explain this?" the man asked the Rav.

With the fervor and simplicity of his *emunah* (faith in Hashem), the Rav answered, "I believe with complete faith that the Creator alone, may His Name be blessed, created, creates, and will create all creations — including the orchard. Because we are fulfilling His will, Hashem showered His blessing on the orchard!"

The years of *orlah* (the initial three years when fruit may not be eaten) passed. The trees were tended like the trees of other orchards. The yearly yield was approximately 700 containers of citrus fruit.

Then the year before *Shemittah* arrived once again. The Jewish Agency staff could not believe the report that came in: That year, Moshav Komemiyus's orchard had yielded more than 2,000 containers of citrus fruit! At first, they suspected a serious counting error. The figures were checked and re-checked — and were proved to be accurate. That year's yield was triple that of every other year!

Once again, they came to the Rav for an explanation. The Rav smiled, opened a *Chumash Vayikra,* and read, "If you will say: What will we eat in the seventh year? — behold! we will not sow and we will not gather our crop! I will ordain My blessing for you in the sixth year and it will yield a crop sufficient for the three years."

The Jewish Agency people, though distant from Torah observance, needed no further explanation. With their own eyes, they had witnessed the fulfillment of the Torah's words!

Faith and Broken Wheat

וְצִוִּיתִי אֶת בִּרְכָתִי לָכֶם
"I will ordain My blessing for you"
(Vayikra 25:21)

R' Binyamin Mendelson, Rav of Moshav Komemiyus, described the difficulty that the moshav had in obtaining wheat seeds for planting after the *Shemittah* year of 5712 (1952). They did not want to use the wheat that had grown during *Shemittah,* and good wheat seedlings from the sixth year were simply not available.

A nearby moshav was prepared to sell them their rejected wheat from the sixth year. This wheat was broken and infested with insects. The Komemiyus resident in charge of the crops came to Rav Mendelson for advice. "What shall we do? There is no good wheat to be had!"

The Rav answered, "If it is impossible to get hold of good wheat that is kosher by halachic standards, then we will place our trust in the Eternal, and Hashem will help by casting His blessing over the broken wheat!"

The news that Moshav Komemiyus had purchased insect-ridden wheat at a high price spread through the area. Residents of the other settlements mocked those of Komemiyus for throwing away their money. They were all certain that not even a single stalk of wheat would grow from such seeds.

R' Yechiel, who was the man in charge of crop cultivation at Komemiyus, followed R' Mendelson's instructions with wholehearted faith in Hashem. Immediately after Sukkos, the fields that had lain fallow all during the seventh year came once again under the plow. Then the broken and insect-ridden wheat was planted in the ground. The plowing and planting took several weeks altogether, bringing them to the middle of winter.

That year, no rain fell until Moshav Komemiyus had finished its planting. The farmers of the nearby settlements, who had already planted their own fields during the summer of the *Shemittah* year, saw their crops shrivel in the ground for lack of rain. But Komemiyus, the single settlement in the region that had delayed its plowing and planting, found itself with a very successful crop!

All saw clearly how Hashem bestows His blessings on those who observe the sanctity of the seventh year — the *Shemittah* year.

A Personal Mission

כִּי יָמוּךְ אָחִיךָ ... וּבָא גֹאֲלוֹ הַקָּרֹב אֵלָיו

"If your brother becomes impoverished ... his redeemer who is closest to him shall come"
(Vayikra 25:25)

One morning, the Kopitshnitzer Rebbe, who lived in the United States, left home to visit one of the men who *davened* in his shul. The man had no idea that the Rebbe was planning to visit. When the Rebbe had been admitted to the house and ushered into the living room, his host rushed to greet him, his jaw slack with astonishment.

"Why has the Rebbe come here?" he blurted. "I could have come to the Rebbe, anywhere and anytime!"

The Rebbe smiled gently, and answered, "Right now, I need you. Therefore, it is appropriate that I come to see you."

"Rebbe," pleaded his host, "please tell me how I can help you."

The Rebbe spoke slowly, his eyes meeting the other man's. "I know a family that is in need of help in the most urgent way. The man is out of work, and his wife, who must be home to take care of their small children, is unable to get a job to help support the family. Several of the children are ill, and there are large medical bills. Even food is difficult for them to buy these days. I need a generous amount of help for them!"

"But if the Rebbe came just for that," his host said, "he could have phoned me. I would certainly have responded to such a request."

"No." The Rebbe shook his head. "We're talking about something very important to me. I wanted to come see you personally."

"I will give the Rebbe whatever amount he asks for."

The Rebbe demurred, explaining that the amount of charity a person gives must be his decision alone.

"Can I give the Rebbe a check?" the other man asked.

"Certainly."

"And to whom shall I make it out?"

The Rebbe looked down for a moment. There was a brief pause before he answered. Then, in a soft voice, he said, "Write out the check to your own poor brother."

A Gerrer chassid in Lodz, who earned his living as a businessman, once approached the Gerrer Rebbe, the *Imrei Emes,* with a request. His business affairs had grown complicated recently and he was having a hard time keeping his head above water financially. He had a brother-in-law, also in Lodz, who was a prosperous businessman and also a Gerrer chassid. The petitioner asked the Rebbe to recommend to this man that he give his brother-in-law a large sum of money as a long-term loan.

The Rebbe listened to the request, then parted from the chassid with a sigh, adding, "Hashem will help you."

The man was taken aback. Afterwards, he asked someone close to the Rebbe to explain what the Rebbe had meant by the heavy sigh. Had he asked the Rebbe something he shouldn't have?

The second man went to the Rebbe for an explanation. The Rebbe answered, "And how could I not sigh? Just a few days ago, the brother-in-law came to me and said that *his* business affairs have grown complicated lately, and asked me to speak to *his* brother-in-law, who was here today, about lending *him* a large sum, so that he could hold his head above water financially."

Refugees

וְאִישׁ כִּי לֹא יִהְיֶה לּוֹ גֹּאֵל
"If a man will have no redeemer"
(Vayikra 25:26)

At the end of World War Two, R' Yaakov Yosef Tabersky of Square settled in Bucharest, the capital city of Romania, and immediately turned his house into a home for the hundreds of refugees who were returning from the concentration camps in search of former homes that were no longer there.

The Rebbe was not satisfied with welcoming everyone who knocked on his door. He also sent his representatives to the train station each day, with instructions to find and bring back anyone who looked Jewish. He would feed them, comfort them, and help them find the means to start a new life. Many of these refugees remained under the Rebbe's roof for months on end.

One of these refugees related: "I was in Auschwitz and stayed alive only through a miracle. When we were freed, I traveled to Bucharest by train, without a clue as to what lay in my future. The moment I got off the train, an unfamiliar Jewish man held out a friendly hand to me and said, '*Shalom aleichem!* The Rebbe sent me to meet you. Here is his address.'

"I had no idea who the Rebbe was, but I had no other place to go. Lacking any other choice, I went to the Rebbe's house. On my arrival, the Rebbe greeted me like a long-lost son. He asked whether I had eaten yet that day, and I said that I hadn't. At once, he led me to the table and served me food and drink. As an afterthought, the Rebbe added, 'You can stay here as long as you want.'"

A Question of Borders

וְשָׁב לַאֲחֻזָּתוֹ
"And he shall return to his ancestral heritage."
(Vayikra 25:27)

The Chasam Sofer was serving as Rav of Matersdorf when a fire broke out in a non-Jew's home. The fire spread, eventually burning down an entire Jewish block. The Chasam Sofer made valiant efforts to rebuild the destroyed houses, in order to provide every person with his own place to live. The entire episode is recorded in his *Teshuvos* (*Yoreh De'ah, siman* 239).

When the rebuilding was launched, numerous arguments erupted. One man would claim, "My property extended to here," while his neighbor objected, "No, only up to here!" The Chasam Sofer devoted a great deal of energy to the division of the property and distribution of the land, until he had allotted each man his proper portion.

One brazen individual went to the city authorities with complaints against the Rav. He claimed that the Chasam Sofer was dividing up the land on his own whim, taking from one to give to the other, without reference to justice or truth. The city authorities came to see the Chasam Sofer and asked him what basis he used in making the division of property.

"How," they asked, "do you know each man's borders?"

The Chasam Sofer picked up an axe and split off an edge of one of the burned-out walls. The bricks at that point faced east-to-west — a clear proof, he said, that this was the house's outer edge. His division was fair and just.

"But how," the judges persisted, "did the Rabbi know this *before* he broke open the wall with that axe?"

The Chasam Sofer showed them the water marks descending from the roof. Such drips, as everyone knows, tend to appear at a house's outer edge. There, again, was proof of the border.

The authorities were amazed at the Chasam Sofer's wisdom and shrewdness — and the entire affair brought about a beautiful *kiddush Hashem* (sanctification of G-d's Name) in the community.

A wealthy Jew once approached the *poritz* in Lantchin, as well as other *poritzim* in the area, proposing that they lease all the inns on their properties to him and let him hire innkeepers to run them as he saw fit. He offered them a good deal and the landowners agreed.

At the appointed time, all the *poritzim* informed their current innkeepers that their tenancy was over and that they must leave the inns. The area's Jewish innkeepers, together with their families and belongings, got together and traveled to Kosov to apprise R' Chaim of the ill tidings that had befallen them.

"Within a short time," the Rebbe promised, "you will all be restored to your former homes and positions."

Meanwhile, the rich Jew placed his own friends in charge of the inns and bought a large quantity of whiskey to sell in the taverns. But when the whiskey was poured for the gentiles, they found it teeming with insects!

The gentile farmers went to the *poritzim* to complain. Disbelieving the tale, the *poritzim* came in person to see the whiskey. To their shock, the story was true! With their own eyes they saw the bugs in the whiskey. The liquor was undrinkable.

The Jewish manager heard the farmers shouting angrily about the insect-ridden drink. Then he got wind of the news that the former innkeepers who were turned away from their posts, had gone to see the Kosover Rebbe. Putting two and two together, he understood that the Rebbe's hand was behind this bizarre phenomenon. He heard, too, that the Rebbe had promised the former innkeepers that they would soon return to their positions. Obviously, if he persisted in opposing the Rebbe's will, he would be afflicted with one trouble after another.

Being an intelligent man, he did not wait for the Ten Plagues to strike him. Instead, he offered the former innkeepers their old jobs and homes back.

The innkeepers, however, were not satisfied. As a group, they demanded fair compensation for the anguish and loss of profits they had suffered when fired from their jobs. They informed the wealthy Jew that he was to come with them to Kosov to see the Rebbe, and he agreed to do so.

"There is a halachah," the Rebbe said, "that fines are not assessed outside of Eretz Yisrael. However, the manager must sell you the whiskey he bought at a very cheap price, as it is infested with bugs." The manager, seeing no use for the insect-infested whiskey, readily agreed.

The innkeepers turned to the Rebbe in confusion. "What," they asked, "are we to do with insect-ridden whiskey? It's not even worth the price we paid, as no one will be willing to drink it!"

The Rebbe smiled. "Do not worry. Return to your homes and sell the whiskey at the normal price. Insect-ridden whiskey — who ever heard of such a thing? Ridiculous!"

And so it was.

Everything Is Remembered

וְכִי יָמוּךְ אָחִיךָ וּמָטָה יָדוֹ עִמָּךְ וְהֶחֱזַקְתָּ בּוֹ

"If your brother becomes impoverished and his hand falters in your proximity, you shall hold on to him"

(Vayikra 25:35)

R' Elazar Menachem Mann Shach related the following story:

When I was once in Vilna, I had the opportunity to look through the community's record book. The book told the story of the Vilna Gaon's wife, who would walk through the streets every *erev Shabbos,* together with a friend, collecting money earmarked for Shabbos necessities for the poor. This was the two women's unchanging custom for many years.

Once, as they walked through the streets of Vilna, they saw a member of the community strolling across the way. He was a man who regularly placed a donation into the kerchief the women held out to him. Seeing him, one of the woman pointed and said, "There's So-and-so." And the two crossed the street to ask the man for his donation.

One day, the friends made a pact. They decided that whoever left this world first would appear to her friend in a dream to tell her what the Next World is like. Eventually, in the course of time, one of them passed away. A little while later she indeed appeared to her friend in a dream.

"You should know this," she said in the dream. "Everything is written down here, and everything is known. Every single thing makes its impact. Do you remember that *erev Shabbos* when we two walked on one side of the street, and I pointed at a certain man on the opposite side of the street, and we both crossed over to ask him for a donation? Well, know this: That pointed finger is written down as a credit to me. And the money we collected from that man is a credit to us both!"

Golda — wife of the great philanthropist, R' Shraga Feivel — once returned home to find, to her shock, that the closet that housed their money had been forced open, the door hanging broken from its hinges. Her husband, R' Shraga Feivel, was at home.

"What happened?" Golda asked.

"A man came asking for a loan. I looked for the key to the closet in order to give him the money, but I couldn't find it. I understood that the key must be with you, or that you had put it away in a different place.

"I thought to myself, 'If I ask the man to come back in two hours when you would be home, saying that I don't know where the key is, he would probably interpret this as an excuse not to give him the loan. He would be distressed and would most likely not return.'

"To tell him to wait until you came home posed another difficulty: I had no idea how long you would be in town. It might be a few minutes, or more than an hour. To sit in the house and wait for you to come so that he might receive the loan would not be pleasant for him, either.

"After thinking it through, I left the room, fetched the iron stick that we use to break the ice, and broke the closet door. It was worth breaking the door, to avoid unpleasantness for a fellow Jew, even for just a few minutes!"

Thirty days after the Chofetz Chaim departed this world, the community gathered together to tell tales of his greatness and holiness. At the start of the evening, community leaders delivered moving eulogies. They called on the people to remember the Chofetz Chaim's behavior and to follow the path he had laid down for them. Afterwards, members of the audience spoke up, telling personal stories of contact with that great man. Nearly everyone there had something to say that he had seen or heard from the Chofetz Chaim.

R' Mottel, the wagon driver, had a particularly interesting story to tell.

"As you know, the Chofetz Chaim often traveled with me. Generally, as we rode along, he would discuss a man's purpose in this world, and the obligations and privileges that he can merit during his lifetime.

"Once," R' Mottel continued, "I asked our Rebbe, 'How can a simple man like me earn life in the World to Come? I hardly have any time to learn Torah, being so busy struggling to support my family. My prayers are the prayers of a simple wagon driver. In that case, how will I merit the World to Come?'

"The Chofetz Chaim answered, 'There is a big change I want you to make. It's not a difficult change, but it will nevertheless earn you all the goodness of both this world and the next! My advice is that you use your money to open a *gemilus chassadim* fund.'

"'But, Rebbe, that would be a joke! I am a poor man, as the Rebbe knows. Often, I myself am in need of a loan from such charitable funds!'

"The Chofetz Chaim explained what he had in mind. 'You mustn't think that a *gemilus chassadim* fund has to be started with a large sum of money. You can help people with small amounts as well. Frequently, a person needs a small sum of money for a short time — and you will be able to help him!

"'Try,' urged the Chofetz Chaim. 'Save a few pennies from your household expenses each week, and when the pennies become gold coins, you'll be able to help your neighbors and friends who need small loans for Shabbos and holiday needs.'

"Gradually, the Chofetz Chaim persuaded me that such a modest fund is no less dear to Hashem than the big funds that loan money to people buying houses and the like.

"He gave me one more suggestion: to put my *ma'aser* money directly into the fund. 'Then you'll be certain that your *ma'aser* money is going to a good place, and you will merit what our Sages, may their memories be blessed, have said: "Give *ma'aser* so that you may become prosperous."'

"And now," concluded R' Mottel, "how happy I am that I followed the Chofetz Chaim's advice. Today I have, *baruch Hashem,* a respectable sum in my fund, and I am able to loan both large and small amounts to dozens of needy people every day!

"I would like to add one thing. Ever since I took care to deposit my *ma'aser* money into the *gemilus chassadim* fund, my income has expanded tremendously. My clientele has grown, and the money that I earn allows me to put a greater sum into my fund, so that it grows ever larger."

One rainy night in Cheshvan, the Tzemach Tzedek of Vizhnitz sat and learned in his inner room, while his assistant lingered in the outer room. Suddenly, the inner door opened. The Rebbe stood in the doorway. "Please get an umbrella and walk into town," he requested. (The Rebbe lived in a house upon a hill, several minutes' walk from the town itself.)

The assistant was frightened. "Please, Rebbe, how will I go out at such a time, in the middle of the night, in the dark?"

Without a word, the Rebbe returned to his room.

About an hour later, the Rebbe appeared again. This time, he held a wad of cash in his hand. "Come what may, you must go. When you see a lit candle, call the man of the house outside, hand him this money, and tell him that I sent you."

The assistant had no choice. He went out into the rain and the wind and groped along the road in the darkness. Every window shutter in town was closed tight — except for one. From a distance, the assistant saw a candle flickering in the night. He walked in the direction of the light, until, with some trepidation, he recognized the house as one belonging to a prosperous businessman.

Stepping up to the window, he heard the man tell his wife that all his wealth had been lost in a bad investment. His business had failed, and he did not have two pennies to rub together.

The Rebbe's assistant understood that this was the place and this was the time. He rapped on the window. When the man stepped outside, the assistant handed him the money in the Rebbe's name, and returned home.

When, in later days, the assistant related this incident (without revealing the businessman's name), he said that he had no idea how much money he handed over that night. All he knew was that the businessman did not go bankrupt, but kept his concern going, and made a success of it. Ever since that night, the businessman was embarrassed to look the assistant in the face.

"The Rebbe," he concluded, "fulfilled the commandment, 'If your brother becomes impoverished and his hand falters in your proximity, you shall hold on to him!'"

R' Tzvi Hirsch of Ziditchov related that, in his youth, he wished to learn to imitate the ways of R' Moshe Leib of Sassov. For that purpose he traveled to R' Moshe Leib's city for the *Yamim Nora'im,* high holy days.

R' Tzvi Hirsch heard from someone in town that the Rebbe "rose up to Heaven" at certain times. One of those times was before saying the *selichos,* "*Zechor HaBris.*" At that time, R' Moshe Leib would disappear from home without anyone seeing him walk out the door. A long while later, he would arrive in shul and begin reciting the *selichos* with tremendous fervor. It was clear to his listeners that he had agitated the heavens Above for sins to be forgiven, and for blessings and redemption in the upcoming new year.

R' Tzvi Hirsch made a mental note of this information. When the time came, he secretly entered the *tzaddik's* room while it was still daylight, and hid in a closet. At midnight, R' Moshe Leib got up, washed his hands, and sat on the ground to recite the *tikkun chatzos* with ashes on his head and tears coursing down his cheeks. Afterwards, he went over to a hidden corner of the house, pulled out farmer's clothing, and put them on. He tied a rope around his waist, and climbed out the window. In this manner, R' Moshe Leib secretly left the house.

R' Tzvi Hirsch hurried after him. A storm was raging outside, and cold flakes of snow stung his face, but he walked rapidly in order not to lose sight of R' Moshe Leib. Through the snow, R' Moshe Leib made his way to the forest at the outskirts of town. He found a dry tree, took an axe from his belt, and began chopping branches from the tree and breaking them into smaller lengths. He used the rope that he had tied around his waist to tie the bundle of wood, loaded it on his back, and began to retrace his steps toward town.

On a dark side street, in a house that was nearly ready to fall down about their heads, there lived a sickly widow with her five small children. It was cold in the house, and the sound of coughing came from every room. R' Moshe Leib hastened into the house to light a fire in the oven. When the fire was blazing, he set a kettle to boil and left the house again. By the time the water was boiling he had returned, with a freshly-baked loaf of bread he had just bought at the baker's. From somewhere else he had procured eggs and milk. He set all the food out on the table, straightened the children's blankets, and quietly left the warm house.

When R' Moshe Leib later arrived at shul and began reciting *selichos,* R' Tzvi Hirsch entered secretly after him. Several chassidim came over and asked if he had witnessed the way R' Moshe Leib rose up to Heaven, as they believed.

"Yes," answered R' Tzvi Hirsch. "Everything they say about R' Moshe Leib is true. But, he is even higher than high. He reaches a place where even angels do not reach."

An Easygoing Boss

וּבְאַחֵיכֶם בְּנֵי יִשְׂרָאֵל אִישׁ בְּאָחִיו לֹא תִרְדֶּה בוֹ בְּפָרֶךְ
"But with your brethren, the Children of Israel — a man with his brother — you shall not subjugate him through hard labor."
(Vayikra 25:46)

R' Nosson Tzvi Finkel, the Alter of Slobodka, once told of sitting in the home of the wealthy philanthropist, R' Shraga Feivel Frank, along with a group of illustrious Torah scholars and community leaders. On the table there rested a bell that was used to summon the maid. When she heard the bell, the maid was supposed to come into the room to see what the guests wanted.

Wishing to serve his guests refreshments, R' Shraga Feivel rang the bell — but no maid came. He rang again several minutes later, with the same results. A third and even fourth ringing also produced no sign of the maid.

His guests were amazed. "Why don't you maintain stricter discipline among your staff?" they asked.

The righteous philanthropist smiled. "That's exactly why I'm happy! Always, I'm wary of stumbling, Heaven forbid, in the Torah's prohibition, 'But with your brethren, the Children of Israel ... you shall not subjugate him through hard labor.'

"When I see that my servants are not afraid of me, I feel reassured."

Pity the Prisoners

לֹא יִרְדֶּנּוּ בְּפֶרֶךְ לְעֵינֶיךָ
"He shall not subjugate him through hard labor in your sight."
(Vayikra 25:53)

It was two years after the outbreak of World War One. R' Yosef Shlomo Kahaneman, who later founded the renowned Ponovizhe Yeshivah, set out for Vilna on a mission of *chesed*.

A short time after his departure, hostilities broke out once again between Russia and Germany, with the result that the Ponovizher Rav found himself under German rule in Vilna, while his family remained under the rule of the Russians.

Two lumber merchants who lived in a quiet village near the Vilna forest persuaded the Rav to remain with them until traveling became less dangerous. The Rav knew that this was a good place of refuge. Nevertheless, it was difficult for him to stay in such an isolated spot. He suggested to the merchants that they open a yeshivah there, and support its students. In this way, he stayed in that village for nearly three years while the friendship between himself and the lumber merchants grew ever deeper.

During this period, thousands of Lithuanian Jews were arrested as "spies" by the conquering Russians. The Jews were thrown into prison, and left there under conditions of near starvation and bitter oppression. Even when the city was once again in German hands, the Jews were not released, but were forced to remain imprisoned and subjugated by hard labor. Hunger and thirst claimed many lives.

The village where the Ponovizher Rav was living was situated near the prison camp. At first, local Jews organized food packages for their imprisoned brothers. After a while, however, they realized that there was little chance of the Jewish prisoners being released any time soon. Who knew how long they would be forced to continue feeding their brothers?

When R' Yosef Shlomo heard about this attitude, he became furious.

"The Rambam writes," he said, "that a prisoner falls into the category of one who is hungry or thirsty to the point that his life is threatened. Anyone who ignores his plight is trespassing on the prohibitions of 'Do not harden your heart,' 'Do not stand over your brother's blood,' and 'He shall not subjugate him through hard labor in your sight.' He is also not fulfilling the mitzvos of 'Open your hand to your brother,' 'And your brother shall live with you,' and 'You shall love your fellow man as yourself' — in addition to many other mitzvos and prohibitions."

After R' Yosef Shlomo preached this message to the local citizenry, he turned urgently to his rich acquaintances and asked them to donate gold coins. Through various complicated stratagems, and at considerable personal risk, the Rav managed to liberate thousands of Jews who were being held hostage — at a ransom of ten rubles per prisoner. He paid his own portion from the partnership he had forged between himself and the lumber merchants.

Rising and Falling

כִּי לִי בְנֵי יִשְׂרָאֵל עֲבָדִים

"For the Children of Israel are slaves to Me"

(Vayikra 25:55)

One year, many of the city of Brody's most prosperous businessmen suffered reversals of fortune that left them poor, while those who worked for them became rich.

Those who had "fallen" went to R' Sholom, the Belzer Rebbe, to complain about their lot.

"This is your punishment," the Rebbe said, "because you worked your people too hard. You have all forgotten what it says in the Torah: 'For the Children of Israel are slaves to Me' — not slaves of slaves."

All Jews Are Equal

כִּי לִי בְנֵי יִשְׂרָאֵל עֲבָדִים עֲבָדַי הֵם אֲשֶׁר הוֹצֵאתִי אוֹתָם מֵאֶרֶץ מִצְרָיִם

"For the Children of Israel are slaves to Me, they are My slaves, whom I have taken out of the land of Egypt"

(Vayikra 25:55)

When R' Yitzchak of Vorka came to Kinchak, he was received with great honor. The head of the community threw a lavish feast in his honor, with great candelabras lighting the house, and ornate rugs on the stairs.

Seeing what was going on, R' Yitzchak refused to come in. "Let them douse the candles and remove the carpets, or else guarantee me that *every* guest to your home will be received in such a style!"

"Why?" his host asked in surprise.

"I am a guest," R' Yitzchak explained. "If you welcome every guest in this manner, I will have to accept this kind of reception. However, if not, I do not want all this."

"But your honor is a *tzaddik* — a great man!" his host persisted.

"We are commanded in the mitzvah of welcoming guests just as we are commanded in the mitzvah of blowing the shofar," R' Yitzchak replied. "Is there a difference between the horn of a small ram or a large one?"

And R' Yitzchak would not enter the house until the candelabras had been doused and the rugs taken away.

The Rabbi Is Watching

אֶת שַׁבְּתֹתַי תִּשְׁמֹרוּ

"My Sabbaths shall you observe"

(*Vayikra* 26:2)

When R' Eliyahu Chaim Meisel was appointed Rav of the city of Lodz, he announced: "As long as I am the Rav here, there will be no *chillul Shabbos* in this city!"

And that's the way it was. All the years that R' Eliyahu Chaim served as Rav of Lodz, no Jew opened his shop on Shabbos.

Once, the Rav was told of a certain Jewish shopkeeper at the edge of town who had begun to open his store on Shabbos. On the following Shabbos, R' Eliyahu Chaim sent word to the congregation of his shul not to wait for him, but to start *davening* on their own. He went to the store on the edge of town, and found it closed. Requesting a chair from the house next door, the Rabbi sat down near the store's door to wait.

A short time later, the Jewish shopkeeper appeared, the shop keys in his hand. When he saw the Rav sitting beside the door, he was filled with shame. The Jew was not brazen enough to desecrate the Shabbos right in front of the Rav's eyes.

"Maybe the Rav was asked to serve as *sandak* at a *bris milah,* and that's why he's waiting here!" the shopkeeper thought. He decided to go back home and return later.

The second time he came, at noon, he saw that R' Eliyahu Chaim had not budged from the spot or returned home to eat his Shabbos meal. The man understood the Rabbi's intentions. The Rabbi had come because of *him* — in order to prevent him from desecrating the Shabbos!

Humbly, he approached the Rav. "Rebbi, I get the hint. I know why the Rav is sitting here all day. Enough. Please, go home and eat. I promise that, from now on, my shop will be closed on Shabbos!"

A merchant came to see R' Yisrael of Alexander. "I manage a store," he said, "but it does not bring me enough income!"

The Rebbe replied, "If you permit me to become a silent partner in your business, and assign to me 15 percent of your profits, your livelihood will be assured."

The man agreed very willingly to these terms, and a contract was drawn up. Afterwards, the Rebbe said, "Now that a seventh of the business belongs to me, I choose the Shabbos as my portion. Any profits from that day will be mine, while the profits of the other six days of the week belong to you. I demand, therefore, that the shop be closed on my day, on the Shabbos. In this merit, you will succeed on the other six days."

The man listened to the Rebbe — and was rewarded with success in his business from that day on.

פרשת בחקתי
Parashas Bechukosai

Standing on Principle

אִם בְּחֻקֹּתַי תֵּלֵכוּ

"If you will go in My decrees"
(Vayikra 26:3)

"That you should be laboring in the Torah." (Rashi)

R' Eliyahu Lopian related the following episode:
During World War One, people were starving for food. All the neighbors sent for their sons who were learning in yeshivah, in order that the boys might find jobs and earn money so the family would have food. Our family had nine sons, all studying in holy yeshivos, but my wife did not want them to leave yeshivah, Heaven forbid, for even an hour.

When the neighboring women saw the state of constant hunger in our home, they asked my wife, "Why do you suffer so? Call two or three of your sons home from yeshivah and send them to work to fend off hunger in your home!"

Forcefully, the Rebbetzin answered, "I don't want my sons to help me now. There will come a time when I will need their help — in *Olam HaEmes*, the World of Truth. I want them to stay in yeshivah now, so that they will be able to help me then, when I will really need them!"

When the Rebbetzin passed away in England (ended R' Lopian), I was the tenth in the *minyan* that accompanied her to her grave. The other nine were our sons, learning *mishnayos* and reciting *Kaddish* for her. She must surely be enjoying *nachas* from her sons today.

R' Aharon Cohen, *Rosh Yeshivah* of Chevron, became sick and required surgery.

"There is no possibility of general anesthesia in this case," warned the operating surgeon. "Putting him to sleep would be too dangerous in the patient's frail state. The operation will have to take place without anesthesia!"

R' Aharon tranquilly agreed to this condition. He only asked for a quarter of an hour's time before they began to operate.

When the 15 minutes had passed, the surgeon started his work. While the scalpel cut into his flesh, R' Aharon marshaled his troops. Like a general marching to battle, he drafted forces from his agile brain: question and answer, Rashi and *Tosafos,* Rambam and Rashba. He lay on the operating table, as peaceful as a man asleep in his own bed at night.

When the surgeon was done, he expressed his amazement. R' Aharon explained: "I was involved in a *sugya* and I didn't feel a thing."

A most holy anesthetic!

R' Shlomo Zalman Auerbach once required a serious and complicated operation, which left him with a loss of hearing in one ear.

On the day of the surgery, his family surrounded him in the hospital. Each face was stamped with worry and tension as their lips murmured snatches of prayer. As R' Shlomo Zalman waited for his operation, he discussed a thorny halachic topic with his brother-in-law, the *gaon* R' Avraham Hurvitz. The two continued their discussion in deep earnest as they walked slowly toward the operating room. Standing at the door, R' Avraham parted from his brother-in-law with a heavy heart, tears coursing from his eyes.

R' Shlomo Zalman stood in the doorway, deep in thought. Then he turned back to his brother-in-law. Heart hammering, R' Avraham stepped nearer. In a calm and confident voice, R' Shlomo Zalman added another thought to the *sugya* they had been discussing.

All around him, the faces were tense and worried, but R' Shlomo Zalman was able to distance himself from human fears by devoting himself, heart and soul, to the Divine work of serving Hashem through the study of His holy Torah!

The Missing Word

וְאֶת מִצְוֹתַי תִּשְׁמְרוּ וַעֲשִׂיתֶם אֹתָם

"And observe My commandments and perform them"

(Vayikra 26:3)

R' Simchah Zissel of Kelm was so weak and frail, that he had to search for a very small *esrog* for Sukkos because a larger one was too heavy for him to hold. His body was not able to sustain even the smallest burden. To prevent himself from fainting, he kept small biscuits near him for quick nourishment.

Despite this great weakness, however, R' Simchah Zissel would spend a long time over his prayers. Having taken upon himself never to *daven* without a siddur, he did not put his siddur down all through the *davening*.

Once, as he *davened Shacharis* in shul, R' Simchah Zissel abruptly stood, walked over to the benches at the back of the room, opened a siddur, and looked inside it for a moment. Then he returned to his place and continued his *davening*.

The explanation for this unusual behavior emerged later. It seemed that R' Simchah Zissel's siddur had been slightly torn, so that one word was missing. Because he had undertaken to always *daven* from a siddur, he stood up, weak as he was, to search for a different siddur so he could read the word!

Satisfied With Little

וַאֲכַלְתֶּם לַחְמְכֶם לָשׂבַע וִישַׁבְתֶּם לָבֶטַח בְּאַרְצְכֶם

"You will eat your bread to satiety and you will dwell securely in your land."

(Vayikra 26:5)

"You will eat your bread to satiety — he will eat a bit, and it will become blessed in his innards." (Rashi)

The Vilna Gaon would tell the story of an old man and his wife from whom he had learned the invaluable trait of being satisfied with little.

During the Gaon's years of self-exile, he once arrived in a small Polish town. As was his custom, he went at once to the *beis midrash* and learned there until morning. After *davening,* he noticed an elderly blind man, wrapped in his *tallis* and *tefillin,* studying and reviewing Torah from memory in a spirit of purity and holiness.

When all the others had left the shul, the old man's wife entered and served him breakfast. The man told her, "You will surely find a holy young man here. I heard him learning sweetly all night long. Please, go to him and ask him to eat with me!"

The woman did as her husband asked, but the Vilna Gaon declined the invitation, saying that there might not be enough for her husband. The woman pressed him to change his mind. Her husband joined in, saying, "Do not worry, your honor. My wife gathers the leftover flour from the grindstones and we eat our fill from that, *baruch Hashem.* We even feed poor people at our table!"

After a great deal of coaxing, the Gaon agreed to join the blind man at his meal.

On Friday, the same old man invited the Vilna Gaon for Shabbos. "My Shabbos table is set like those of respected homeowners," he said, and went on to describe the source of their food supply. "Before Shabbos, my wife works at removing feathers from the chickens in the slaughterhouses. In return, she receives the chickens' heads and feet, with which she prepares a good Shabbos meal. She uses the remaining flour that she gathered from the grindstones to bake challahs."

Once again, the Gaon found it impossible to refuse. At the couple's Shabbos table sat important guests, clearly enjoying themselves. The old man sat beaming radiantly, the *Shechinah* resting on him.

Each time the Vilna Gaon would tell this story he would add, in his own humility, that ever since that time, he had worked to be satisfied with little just like that couple, but had not yet attained that level.

A grandson of R' Yosef Chaim Sonnenfeld related the following incident:

After my grandfather married his second wife, I once came to his house and smelled a delicious chicken soup. I sat beside him and began to tell him about my *Rosh Yeshivah's* latest *shiur*.

While we were talking, the Rebbetzin came in and set down a bowl of steaming soup. My grandfather picked up his spoon, dipped it into the soup, and brought it to my lips, saying, "Taste it, my son, taste it! It will no doubt taste delicious to you."

After that, my grandfather took a single spoonful of soup himself — and no more.

When his wife returned to the room, he began to praise her expert cooking, then added apologetically, "Forgive me, but such delicacies on a weekday are a little too much. All my life, I have been careful not to indulge my body and have accustomed myself to being satisfied with little. In that case, why ruin it near the end of my life, when I am close to leaving my body?

"Save the dish for Shabbos," R' Yosef Chaim continued, "then I will be thrilled to enjoy your wonderful food, and will taste it with great pleasure!"

R' Yosef Chaim was 78 years old then, ill and weak after many years of suffering, first through his first wife's illness, then nine years of widowhood. He certainly was in need of nourishment. But he had always trained his body to make do with little. To indulge it now, in the autumn of his life, seemed a foolish idea.

But in honor of Shabbos, such enjoyment was a mitzvah, not an indulgence. This kind of pleasure belongs not to the body, but to the soul.

The Miracle

וְהִפְרֵיתִי אֶתְכֶם וְהִרְבֵּיתִי אֶתְכֶם וַהֲקִימֹתִי אֶת בְּרִיתִי אִתְּכֶם

"I will make you fruitful and increase you; and I will establish My covenant with you."

(*Vayikra* 26:9)

Many years before the Vilna Gaon was born, Hashem guarded the precious soul that was preparing to descend to earth. A young woman in Seltz crossed a bridge that spanned a river. In her arms, lying on a pillow, was her infant daughter.

Suddenly, the woman's foot slipped on the bridge. Pillow and baby flew out of her arms and into the waters below. The other people on the bridge, witnesses to this horrifying sight, despaired for the child's life. No one dared leap into the deep water to rescue her.

Then, to their amazement, they saw the pillow floating on the water, the baby resting securely on it.

The infant was eventually pulled out of the river and hurried, along with her mother, to a nearby house to warm up. A fire was lit in the oven for the shivering baby — who was accidentally placed on its searing surface. Though the tiny girl's legs were badly burned, her life was miraculously spared.

The child's name was Traina, and she grew up to marry R' Shlomo Zalman. From his youth, R' Shlomo Zalman labored in the tents of Torah. He married and fathered a son named Eliyahu, who became the Vilna Gaon.

When R' Chaim of Volozhin, the Vilna Gaon's foremost student, crossed that same bridge many years later, he recited an emotional blessing: "*Baruch she'asah li nes bamakom hazeh* — Blessed [is He] Who performed a miracle for me on this spot."

R' Chaim explained that, if not for that miracle, he would not have been privileged to learn Torah from the Gaon, and his life would have been utterly different.

The Policeman and the Drunkard

וְנָתַתִּי מִשְׁכָּנִי בְּתוֹכְכֶם

"I will place my Tabernacle among you"

(*Vayikra* 26:11)

During the reign of Franz Yosef, Emperor of Austria, a certain drunkard's case became notorious throughout the land. The man would walk, inebriated, through the streets of Vienna, occasionally falling into the doorways of shops lining the street. One night, a passing policeman suspected the man of trying to break into a store. He called to the drunkard to stop, but in his intoxication the man did not understand the order.

Again, the policeman warned, "In the name of the law and the king, stop at once ... or I'll shoot!" But, again, the drunkard paid no attention.

Three times the officer shouted his warning, but the drunkard didn't listen. Finally, the policeman shot him in the legs.

After receiving medical treatment for his injuries, the drunkard sued the policeman. At the trial, the officer of the law claimed that he had repeatedly warned the other man, and only shot at him when his warnings were ignored.

The judge was not impressed. He declared that it had been wrong to shoot the man, because he was drunk and therefore unable to comprehend what was being shouted at him.

This infuriated the police officer. "When something is shouted in the name of the king and his law, even the drunkest person in the world should sober up!"

The Jews of the time added a relevant postscript to this story: Every Jew is tested to see how he "sobers up" from the frivolousness of his life when he hears *Shem Shamayim,* the Name of Heaven.

Compassion

וְהִתְהַלַּכְתִּי בְּתוֹכְכֶם

"I will walk among you"

(Vayikra 26:12)

A chassid once came to see R' Baruch of Mezibozh for the first time. He entered the shul in a state of great tension and fear, feeling unprepared to meet the great *tzaddik*.

R' Baruch was in the shul. Seeing the tense and distressed chassid, he came over and asked, "Reb Yid, tell me, why are you so upset?"

"I've come to see R' Baruch, and I heard that he is very strict. When he meets me, he will be very hard on me."

"I know R' Baruch very well," the Rebbe said. "And I know that he is not hard on his chassidim at all."

Taking the chassid's arm, the Rebbe began to stroll around the shul with him until it was time to *daven*.

As soon as the *davening* began, the chassid discovered that the man who had spoken to him and strolled with him was none other than R' Baruch himself. A great trepidation filled his heart because he had walked with the Rebbe without the proper decorum. After *davening,* he entered the Rebbe's room and respectfully begged his forgiveness.

"I am prepared to forgive you," R' Baruch replied with a smile, "but only on one condition: that you come out with me and take another stroll around the shul, the way we did before."

The *tzaddik,* R' Yisrael of Ruzhin, sat in his *sukkah* with his family on the first night of Sukkos. The *sukkah* was beautifully decorated and the table laden with food and drink served on gold and silver platters. Numerous candles shed their festive light over all.

As they sat at their meal, the *sukkah* door suddenly opened and a poor Jewish man burst in. Seeing the bright light and the many people seated around the table, he stood blinking in the doorway, dazed and transfixed.

"Why do you stand there?" called the Rebbe. "Is it beneath your dignity to sit in my *sukkah*? Come, make *Kiddush* and join us!"

And the befuddled Jew stepped hesitantly to the table, never having dreamed that he would merit the honor of sitting in a *sukkah* together with the illustrious *tzaddik*.

The Apology

וְאִם לֹא תִשְׁמְעוּ לִי וְלֹא תַעֲשׂוּ אֵת כָּל הַמִּצְוֹת הָאֵלֶּה

"But if you will not listen to Me and will not perform all of these commandments"

(Vayikra 26:14)

R' Shlomo of Radomsk was a wise and forceful Rav of his community. Afraid of no man, he kept a vigilant guard over the city's spiritual life.

Once, members of the community came to him and related that there was a *moser* living among them — a Jew who went to the gentile authorities with accusations against his fellow Jews. R' Shlomo asked for the man to be brought before him.

When the man arrived, R' Shlomo began to lecture him about the severity of his actions. The man stood and listened quietly until the Rav had finished. Then he left and returned to his own home.

Only a few days later, the others returned to R' Shlomo to complain that the *moser* was continuing in his atrocious behavior. Apparently, the Rav's words of rebuke had fallen on deaf ears. R' Shlomo summoned him again.

"Please, forgive me!" R' Shlomo said the moment the man walked in.

The *moser* was stunned. The Rav continued, "Forgive me for shouting at you and humiliating you the last time you were here. Forgive me!"

Everyone who was present felt the same amazement at these words. The *moser* himself asked R' Shlomo what he meant by them.

"Listen," R' Shlomo explained. "The first time, I thought that my words of rebuke would take root in your heart and bear fruit. If that had happened, there would have been no need to apologize. On the contrary, I would have done you a great favor.

"However, seeing as you are continuing in your horrible behavior, it turns out that I humiliated you for nothing. Therefore, I am obligated to ask your forgiveness."

These logical and sensible words pierced the man's heart like an arrow. At once, he promised R' Shlomo to repent from his evil ways.

In a Hurry

וְנַסְתֶּם וְאֵין רֹדֵף אֶתְכֶם

"You will flee but there will be no one pursuing you."

(Vayikra 26:17)

Not feeling well one evening, R' Elchonon Wasserman, *Rosh Yeshivah* of Baranovitch, asked a group of his students to come to his house to *daven Ma'ariv* that night. One of the youths — a student who had joined the yeshivah just a short time before — asked to serve as the *shaliach tzibbur*.

The boy had not yet accustomed himself to the slow pace of *davening* at the yeshivah. He was used to *davening* more quickly, as was done in the neighborhood shuls in his home town. Several times during *Ma'ariv,* as the youth hurried along, R' Elchonon Wasserman lifted his head to look at him, his gaze both surprised and troubled. It was clear that the boy had no concept of the way *tefillah* was meant to be said — and especially, the *tefillos* of yeshivah *bachurim*.

When the *davening* was over, R' Elchonon motioned the youth over to him. First he asked the student's name and where he was from. Then the *Rosh Yeshivah* said gently, "I wanted you to know that the *pasuk,* 'You will flee but there will be no one pursuing you,' is part of the *tochachah* (rebuke) that Moshe Rabbeinu delivered to *Klal Yisrael!*"

R' Elchonon's admonition, delivered so gently, left a lasting impression on the more mature *bachurim,* who got the hint. Prayers recited hurriedly, without any thought for the meaning of the words, appear to *Hakadosh Baruch Hu* like a senseless fleeing from nonexistent enemies!

Bechukosai / 195

The Best Preventative

וְאִם עַד אֵלֶּה לֹא תִשְׁמְעוּ לִי וְיָסַפְתִּי לְיַסְּרָה אֶתְכֶם

"And if during these you will not heed Me, I will increase tormenting you"

(Vayikra 26:18)

A certain city in Lithuania held a meeting whose aim was the establishment of a Jewish hospital. Leading the meeting was the Chofetz Chaim.

Among the participants were several prosperous businessmen, each of whom committed himself to donating money to the new hospital. One man promised to pay for one hospital bed, while others guaranteed to pay for several beds. The Chofetz Chaim took note of these donations and honored the men as though they were performing a *chesed* of inestimable value.

There were also several yeshivah students at the meeting, and the Chofetz Chaim honored them greatly, too. This angered one of the businessmen, who thought to himself, "How can it be? We are giving a lot of money, yet he honors *them* as well?"

He stood up and asked the Chofetz Chaim with visible annoyance, "How many beds did these yeshivah students donate?"

Promptly, the Chofetz Chaim answered, "They donated fifty beds each!"

"Fifty beds? But — but that represents an enormous amount of money! Each of us, with all our income, only gave ten beds at the most ... and they gave fifty?"

The Chofetz Chaim explained. "Each one of these yeshivah students has saved us the expense of fifty beds! The Torah protects and succors, and the Torah that these young men are learning keeps illness and trouble away from many people, so we don't need hospital beds for them!"

Suspicion

וְיָסַפְתִּי עֲלֵיכֶם מַכָּה שֶׁבַע כְּחַטֹּאתֵיכֶם

"Then I shall lay a further blow upon you — seven, like your sins."

(Vayikra 26:21)

The two holy brothers, R' Elimelech and R' Zusha, spent a period of their lives wandering from town to town. Arriving in a certain village, they stayed overnight at an inn, then rose early in the morning and set out on the road again.

That same night, two horses were stolen from that inn. When daylight broke and the landlord noticed the missing horses, his suspicions fell immediately on the brothers.

"It was surely those two who stole the horses! That's why they hurried away from here so early, before the theft was discovered!"

He ran out at once and chased after the brothers, until he came upon them walking slowly along the road.

"Where are my horses?" he shouted.

The brothers walked quietly along, not saying a word.

"Why did you steal my horses?" the host screamed, even louder.

Again, the two didn't answer. The host took their silence as an admission of guilt. In a fury, he began raining blows upon them. The blows were cruel and extremely painful, but the brothers received them with love. If justice called upon them to suffer, they would suffer gladly.

After beating them energetically, the host left the brothers alone. Only then did R' Elimelech turn to R' Zusha and say, "See, my brother, how great is the punishment for sinners. We, who have not stolen but are only suspected of it, suffered a grievous beating. Imagine the punishment that actual thieves will receive from the Heavenly Court, when they stand up to face the judgment for their sins!"

A Cup of Tears

וְנָתַתִּי אֶת עָרֵיכֶם חָרְבָּה וַהֲשִׁמּוֹתִי אֶת מִקְדְּשֵׁיכֶם

"I will put your cities to ruin and I will make your sanctuaries desolate"

(Vayikra 26:31)

R' Moshe Normista, who, before moving to Jerusalem, was frequently at the home of the Chasam Sofer, told this story:

"Once, on the afternoon of *erev Tishah B'Av,* the Chasam Sofer went alone into a special room. I was very curious to know why he wished to be alone, as I knew that on the afternoon of *erev Tishah B'Av* one does not engage in *halachah* or in writing answers to people who have asked halachic questions.

"I gathered my courage and peeked through a crack in the door. What an awesome sight I saw! That man of G-d was sitting and crying over the destruction of the *Beis Hamikdash*. Nearby rested a *sefer,* and his hand held a cup into which he let his tears fall, until it was filled with tears!

"Later, as the Chasam Sofer sat down to eat the *seudah hamafsekes* (the last meal before the fast), he sipped from the cup of tears, to fulfill the verse, 'Feed them bread of tears and give them tears to drink.'"

One *erev Tishah B'Av,* after eating the *seudah hamafsekes,* R' Levi Yitzchak of Berditchev went over to his window and stood motionless, gazing out. He stood there for a long time, until the people had already gathered to hear Megillas Eichah. Then his assistant came over and whispered, "Rebbe, the people are waiting."

R' Levi Yitzchak lifted his eyes. "What? Hasn't the *Mashiach* come yet?"

"He has not yet come," the other answered soberly.

R' Levi Yitzchak ran to the shul, fell onto the ground, and burst into bitter weeping: "*Eichah yashvah badad* — How does Yerushalayim sit in solitude."

When the time came to write up the *Tena'im* at his granddaughter's engagement, in which was written the proposed date of the wedding in Berditchev, R' Levi Yitzchak tore up the paper and ordered that the following be written in its place:

"The wedding will take place, *im yirtzeh Hashem* and with *mazal tov*, in the holy city of Yerushalayim. And if, Heaven forbid, the *Mashiach tzidkeinu* does not come this year, the wedding will take place in Berditchev."

Special Status

אַךְ בְּכוֹר אֲשֶׁר יְבֻכַּר לַד' בִּבְהֵמָה ... לַד' הוּא

"However, a firstborn that will become a firstling for Hashem among livestock ... it is Hashem's."

(*Vayikra* 27:26)

R' Avraham of Chechenov's scrupulousness with respect to *kashrus* was legendary. When calves were brought in from the surrounding villages for slaughter, the Rebbe would interrogate the men accompanying the livestock to find out whether the calves were at least eight days old, as required by Jewish law.

Once, a calf's lung was brought to him for inspection. The lung was extremely smooth, without the slightest flaw or bump. Nevertheless, R' Avremele decreed, "It is too nice," and sent for the butcher. Eventually, he learned from the butcher that the calf's mother had been sold to a non-Jew before giving birth. R' Avremele asked to see the bill of sale — and found it legally invalid. The calf was thus a firstborn animal, a *bechor* — and the Rebbe ordered it buried in accordance with Jewish law.

The Tenth Man

הָעֲשִׂירִי יִהְיֶה קֹדֶשׁ לַד'
"The tenth one shall be holy to Hashem."
(Vayikra 27:32)

One *erev Yom Kippur* afternoon found R' Leib Sara's stranded in a certain village, unable to continue on his way. He understood that there was an important purpose for his being in that place on that particular day. He found a Jew and asked whether there was a *minyan* for the Yom Kippur services in the village.

"We are only eight," the villager answered. "You can be the ninth, and two Jewish men are supposed to be coming here before evening from a neighboring village."

When the holiday began, the *minyan* gathered to say *Kol Nidrei* — and found, to their dismay, that the two Jews from the nearby village had been arrested. They were left without a quorum for *davening*.

"Isn't there any other Jew here — even a non-believer?" asked R' Leib. I have heard from my teachers that even if one scratches in the dirt one can find a spark of fire."

The villagers told him that the *poritz,* the landlord of the entire village, was a Jew who had converted and married the previous *poritz's* daughter. He had lived a sinful life for the past forty years. The wife had since passed away and the couple had had no children, so the nobleman lived alone in his palace.

R' Leib asked to be shown the *poritz's* mansion. The others reluctantly agreed, though they were anxious lest their landlord's wrath should fall upon their heads. R' Leib removed his *tallis.* Wearing his white *kittel,* he walked up the path leading to the *poritz's* home.

Arriving at the palace, R' Leib entered immediately, without asking permission, and stood before the stunned nobleman. The thought crossed the convert's mind to summon his servants and have them throw the intruder into a deep pit in his courtyard. But R' Leib's countenance was shining like an angel's, and the *poritz's* heart was softened.

"My mother, Sarah," R' Leib said, "was a pure and righteous

Jewish woman who married an elderly Jew in order to save herself from marriage to the *poritz*. You, on the other hand, have not withstood your own challenge, and for the price of gold and silver have abandoned your faith. But know this: There are men who 'purchase their World to Come in a single hour!' *And this is your hour!*"

R' Leib's voice was soft and persuasive. "It is now Yom Kippur eve, and the Jews in your village are missing one man for a *minyan*. Come join us. The verse says, 'The tenth one shall be holy to Hashem.'"

A short time later, the shul door opened. In walked R' Leib, and behind him walked the *poritz*! He was handed a *tallis*, which he placed over his head. R' Leib took two Torah scrolls out of the ark, gave the first to one of the elderly Jews in the *minyan* and the other to the *poritz*. Then he began reciting, in the age-old traditional melody, "With the permission of the Creator and the permission of this congregation ... we are permitted to pray with sinners."

A deep, shuddering sigh burst from the *poritz*. The others were shaken at the sound, and broke into tears. All through *Ma'ariv,* and throughout the following day, from *Shacharis* to *Ne'ilah*, the *poritz* stood on his feet, wrapped in the *tallis* — a shattered and humbled man sighing deeply from the depths of his heart and weeping as one who is heartbroken.

When *Ne'ilah* was over and they reached the point where the *Shema Yisrael* is said, the *poritz* walked over to the holy ark, stuck his head inside, and embraced the *sifrei Torah* there. In a clear, loud voice he recited the *Shema Yisrael* and *Baruch Shem*. Then he removed his head from the *aron kodesh,* stood erect, and cried out with all his might, "*Hashem Hu HaElokim!* — Hashem is the L-rd!" seven times. With each repetition, his voice grew louder — until he cried out the words for the seventh time. At that instant, with the word "*Elokim,*" his soul departed this earth and returned to its Creator.

The onlookers were awe-struck upon witnessing this scene. However, once again, they were left without a *minyan* for *Ma'ariv.*

R' Leib ruled, "With his heartfelt repentance he has purified himself of all his sins and transformed himself into a complete *tzaddik*. In their deaths, *tzaddikim* are called alive."

From that day, R' Leib kept the custom of reciting *Kaddish* every Yom Kippur for the soul of that *ba'al teshuvah*.

The Bad and the Good

לֹא יְבַקֵּר בֵּין טוֹב לָרַע

"He shall not distinguish between good and bad"

(Vayikra 27:33)

A poor Jew once came to see R' Nachum of Chernobyl. He had a daughter of marriageable age, he said sadly, but no money with which to see her married. R' Nachum had the sum of fifty coins at the time, and gave them at once to the poor man, along with his own silk garments.

That poor man enjoyed drinking to the point of drunkenness. With the money in hand, he went at once to the tavern and began drinking as usual.

The Rebbe's *gabbaim,* seeing that R' Nachum had given away all the money he had, followed the poor man to see what he did with it. When they saw him drinking in the tavern, they took the remaining money away from him and dragged him back to the Rebbe, where they related what the drunkard had done.

R' Nachum said in a clear, forceful voice, "I heard them announce in the Upper World that Nachum of Chernobyl clings to *Hakadosh Baruch Hu's* trait of bestowing good on people both bad and good. And you wish to steal this from me? Quickly return the clothes and the money to that man and let him go!"